THE UNPUBLISHED
SPIKE MILLIGAN

BOX
18

Also published by Fourth Estate:

The Essential Spike Milligan
edited by Alexander Games

The Compulsive Spike Milligan
edited by Norma Farnes

Spike: An Intimate Memoir
by Norma Farnes

THE UNPUBLISHED SPIKE MILLIGAN

BOX 18

Edited by
Norma Farnes

FOURTH ESTATE • London

First published in Great Britain in 2006 by Fourth Estate

An imprint of HarperCollinsPublishers
77–85 Fulham Palace Road
London W6 8JB
www.4thestate.co.uk

A catalogue record for this book is available from the British Library
ISBN 13: 978-0-00-721427-3
ISBN 10: 0-00-721427-8

Typeset and designed by Estuary English

Printed in Great Britain by Butler & Tanner, Frome

This book is for my mentor and friend
Lawrence Drizen

ACKNOWLEDGMENTS

I would like to thank Janet Spearman for her help
not just with this book but over the years; Louise
Haines, my editor, who always has faith in me;
Alan ('Groucho') Matthews, a true Milligan fan;
Eric Sykes, for always being there; Joan Taylor, my
mother's angel; Pamela Lester, for all her support
over the years; and for just being him,
Bill Kenwright.

Special thanks to Jack Clarke for his
encouragement, support and love.

EDITOR'S NOTE

I have called this book *The Unpublished Spike Milligan*, and that's what it is. If anything has slipped through the net and has been published before, *mea culpa* – but please, please: no letters of complaint saying you've seen it before. I did my best. If the old sod were here he'd say, 'That's what worries me.'

CONTENTS

INTRODUCTION 15
SPIKE'S DIARIES 23
SCRIPTS FOR
"MILLIGAN'S MILLENNIUM" 45
HERMAN GORING 71
STORIES FOR CHILDREN 85
VERY BAD JELLY 109
A MILLIGAN MISCELLANY 123
TREE MANIAC 153
SPIKE'S LETTERS 173

Fame at last.

INTRODUCTION

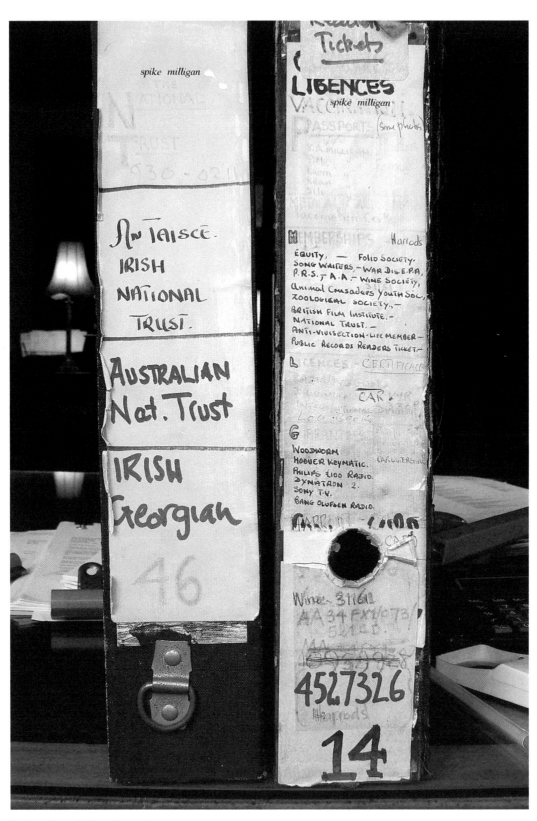

Spike's list of files (Box 14).

BOX 18 – IDEAS. An extraordinary title, but then Spike was an extraordinary man. His public persona was that of a manic, scatty, undisciplined character, someone who spoke with machine-gun delivery, a thoroughly disorganised individual. This was the complete opposite of Spike in the office; he was the most focused person I have ever met: disciplined, methodical and meticulous about his filing system. Yes – his filing system: large box files for his office work, fourteen and a half inches by ten and a half, numbered 1, 2, 3, 4, etc. Then his household files were ten inches by seven and a half inches, marked a, b, c, d, etc. The labels on the files were in his own calligraphy handwriting, describing what they contained, all except Box 1, which quite simply bore the title 'Files'. This contained one piece of paper listing all the box files and their contents. For example:

Box 18 – Ideas. This contained Spike's ideas. He would scribble a poem and put it in this file. Sometimes it would be incomplete and he would work on it, perhaps a week or a month later, or it would be 'chucked'. The file contained ideas for speeches, stories or sketches for one of his television programmes. Sometimes we would sit and go through them together – and, of course, he would occasionally say, 'I'll bin that. I didn't realise I could be that unfunny.' The longest 'idea' was a children's story called 'The Magic Staircase'. It was in the file for about three years. He would take it out, look at it, put it back and say, 'I like this. It's a good idea. I'll keep it.' One day he took it out of the file and said, 'Today's the day for "The Magic Staircase".' He worked on it for two weeks, by which time it was a novel mixing fact and fiction. It was published in 1990 under the title *It Ends With Magic* and is, in my opinion, Spike's most skilled piece of writing.

One thing never ceased to amaze me: when he decided to work on any one of his ideas he would sit at the typewriter and the writing simply flowed. He really was blessed with a natural gift. Now, having explained Spike's meticulous filing system, every now and then the other Spike would emerge. He'd have a tantrum and want something from one of his files NOW. He would take out whatever he needed and, when he had finished with it, throw it in the bin. So the next time he needed it and it wasn't there, someone had 'fucked up my filing system'. Or, when he was manic, he would for no apparent reason decide to rearrange two or three of the files, or to amalgamate them. He'd stick pieces of paper over the existing meticulous piece of paper, in some cases covering up the list of contents. That's when the trouble would start – and, believe me, this was not infrequent. When the storm was over he would sit quietly and start all over again; it was ever so.

The idea for this book came to me when I was looking for a story that Spike had written. He called it a 'life after death story'. It was a particular favourite of mine and I thought his writing had really captured the essence of life after death. It had been an idea for a radio programme and I had wanted to include it, together with some other stories, in a book entitled *Short Stories by Spike Milligan*. I thought it was too good to lay fallow in Box 18. But, as always, other ideas captured Spike's imagination and it would be, 'Promise, Norm – next time.' Then he eventually did write another story – 'The Bing Bong Circus' – and I foolishly thought we were on the way, yet again. Not to be: 'Bing Bong' was added to Box 18.

My favourite of all the children's books was *Badjelly the Witch*, and I tried to persuade him on several occasions to write a follow-up. Again, it was started and added to – and ended up you know where. Trying to persuade Spike to do something when he wasn't in the mood was like 'swimming in porridge' (one of his expressions). So, to encourage him, I asked him to draw a Badjelly, a dragon and a castle. He did. Progress! He sent it to me and it wasn't one of his best efforts, either in order to shut me up or a case of 'That's the best I can do and that's that.' I sent it back to him with a note saying, '6/10. Could do better. Talk to me.' He did. He sent it back and, sure enough, it had indeed been one of the occasions on which 'That's the best I can do and that's that.' So why wasn't it thrown away? Kismet. You know what? I've become so fond of that drawing that it makes me smile every time I see it, so I've included it in this book.

While I was in the middle of smiling and reflecting on that incident, I recalled some of the quirky drawings he had done for his poetry books. I looked through them – nostalgia, I suppose – and that's when I realised that they'd make great greetings cards. I approached my favourite card company, Woodmansterne, who were enthusiastic and have since printed a selection of his drawings – though not, of course, the badly drawn dragon, which was returned to the Ideas file.

And it was then that I wondered: would a publisher be interested in a volume of unpublished works by Spike? Louise Haines, Spike's editor, was enthusiastic. I had only intended to publish the Ideas file, but I then recalled all the letters he had written. In my opinion, those I have included show the various facets of Spike's personality, a personality inherited from his mother. I told Spike that if I had a vision of one woman who had built the British Empire, it was his mother. Like her son she was an avid letter writer and wrote to me almost every week for over twenty years. So, to give an insight into her character, I've included just one of her letters. She would have liked that.

Some years ago, when I started to write *Spike: An Intimate Memoir*, Spike gave me his diaries – 'to help you, because you are no bloody good at keeping diaries, so if I give you mine it will keep you off my back. Otherwise it will be, "Do you remember this, Spike?" or "When did we do that, Spike?"' So I've also included some pages from his diaries that I hope will show what a complex and captivating man he was, and give you some idea of his energy and the multitude of activities he could and did embrace in any one day.

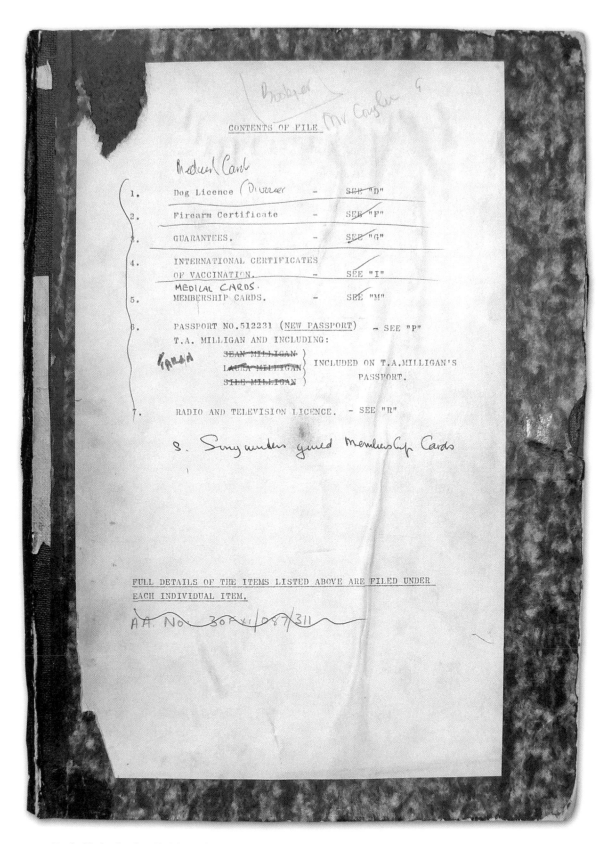

Brodgan *Mr Coyle* "G"

CONTENTS OF FILE

Medical Cards

1.   Dog Licence *(Diurrier*   —   SEE "D"

2.   Firearm Certificate   —   SEE "F"

3.   GUARANTEES.   —   SEE "G"

4.   INTERNATIONAL CERTIFICATES
        OF VACCINATION.   —   SEE "I"

        MEDICAL CARDS.
5.   MEMBERSHIP CARDS.   —   SEE "M"

6.   PASSPORT NO.512231 (NEW PASSPORT)   — SEE "P"
        T.A. MILLIGAN AND INCLUDING:

KAREN   ~~JEAN MILLIGAN~~
        ~~LAURA MILLIGAN~~   INCLUDED ON T.A.MILLIGAN'S
        ~~SILE MILLIGAN~~   PASSPORT.

7.   RADIO AND TELEVISION LICENCE. — SEE "R"

    8. *Songwriters guild Membership Cards*

FULL DETAILS OF THE ITEMS LISTED ABOVE ARE FILED UNDER
EACH INDIVIDUAL ITEM.

A.A. No 30Axi/087/311

Each file had a detailed list of exactly what was inside.

Some of Spike's files.

TRADESMEN
MADE IN ENGLAND
EAST-LIGHT
Receipts
Stewart Stone
Ltd
Laundry
Dry Cleaning.

from........................19....
to........................19....

F

WHEN RE-ORDERING THIS FILE SPECIFY
LOCKSPRING BOX
8vo size
B.E.L.L. Barking & London. LABEL COPYRIGHTED.

MADE IN ENGLAND
EAST-LIGHT
Receipts
PATENT
BOX-FILE
WITH
LOCKSPRING

School fees
" meals
" Travel

from........................19....
to........................19....

N

WHEN RE-ORDERING THIS FILE SPECIFY
LOCKSPRING BOX
8vo size
B.E.L.L. Barking & London. LABEL COPYRIGHTED.

TRADESMEN
MADE IN ENGLAND
EAST-LIGHT
RECEIPTS
PATENT
BOX-FILE
WITH
LOCKSPRING

Car Hire
Garages.
Petrol, Oil, Etc

from....April.....19....
to........................19....

Receipts P

WHEN RE-ORDERING THIS FILE SPECIFY
LOCKSPRING BOX
8vo size
B.E.L.L. Barking & London. LABEL COPYRIGHTED.

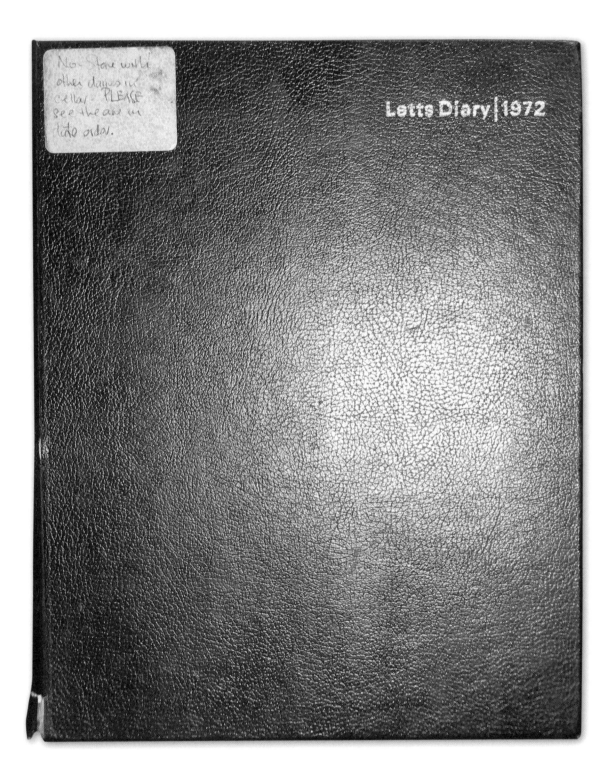

The sticker in the top left corner reads: 'Now store with other diaries in cellar. PLEASE see the(y) are in date order.'

SPIKE'S DIARIES

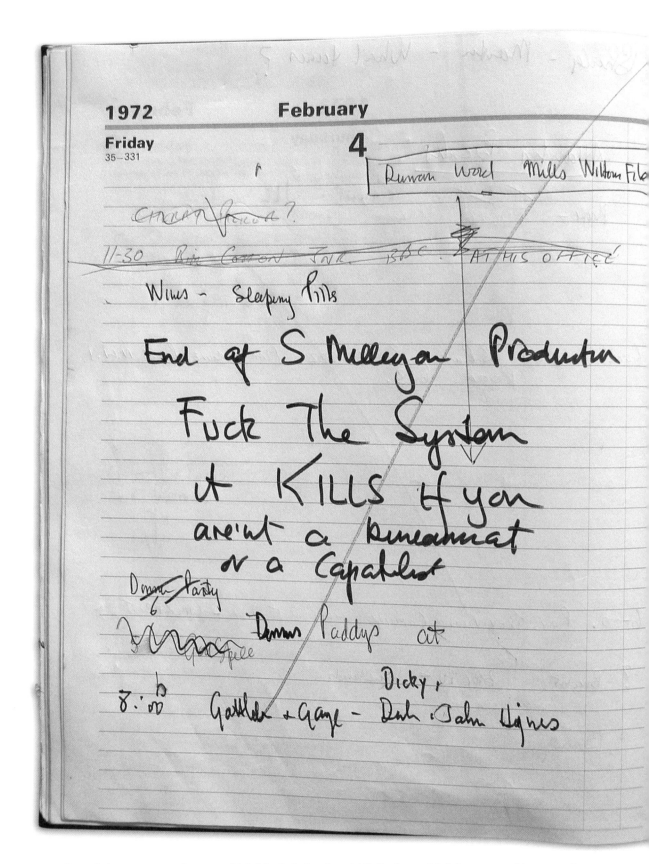

1972   **February**

Friday
35–331

4

Ruman Word Mills Wilton Film

Charnford?

11-30 Ria Cotton Jak. BBC. AT HIS OFFICE

Wines - Sleeping Pills

End of S Milligan Production

Fuck The System

it KILLS if you
are'nt a Beauocrat
or a Capitalist

Dinner Party

Dinner Paddys at

Dicky.
8:00 Gabbler + Gaye - Dah. John Hignes

One of the many occasions on which I had obviously told Spike he couldn't have something out of the company. It was the end for him – but not for the company, which is still in existence today.

Sale £5 - 80.

① See Laura give her B+W Drawing out fits.
② Hardware - wuks
③

Say 2.00   bcc 9 Ome
14.30. 2.30
STEVE WILL PICK YOU UP. AT 127 HOLDEN ROAD.
~~#4 30 HRS~~ .
4-5. PLANE. FLIGHT No. BE. 926.
     ARRIVE. 5-5 DUBLIN.

5-5. MET AT AIRPORT BY MIKE McWEENY
Hiberman

Ⓟ

IRISH TV. Details later Tell Paddy.
I was told the who programme was
turned over to me to I read my
book — on arrival I was told this
was not so — They would say I was
in Dublin to sign — then another Author
would talk about his book — HANCOCK.
Peter "Measles" Sellers is also on
the programme.
Went to dinner with Peter Sellers — then Mrs Seller
Sent her Chauffeur — and two TV luas

SIGN BOOKS IN IRELAND. WHAT SHOP?
WHAT ADDRESS!

12-00 UNTIL 2-00 P.M. SIGN BOOKS.
Easons - O'Connel St nx to Metropole

4-40. LEAVE DUBLIN. FLIGHT No. BE. 929.
ARRIVE LONDON. 5-40pm.

STEVE WILL PICK YOU UP.
Ⓟ Tell Paddy
Ⓟ Prepare for Hospital

Pyjyma
Toilet
4 Underpants?
Nuper caudal ?   Ash Ivor Robson

Packing his bag methodically to go into hospital.

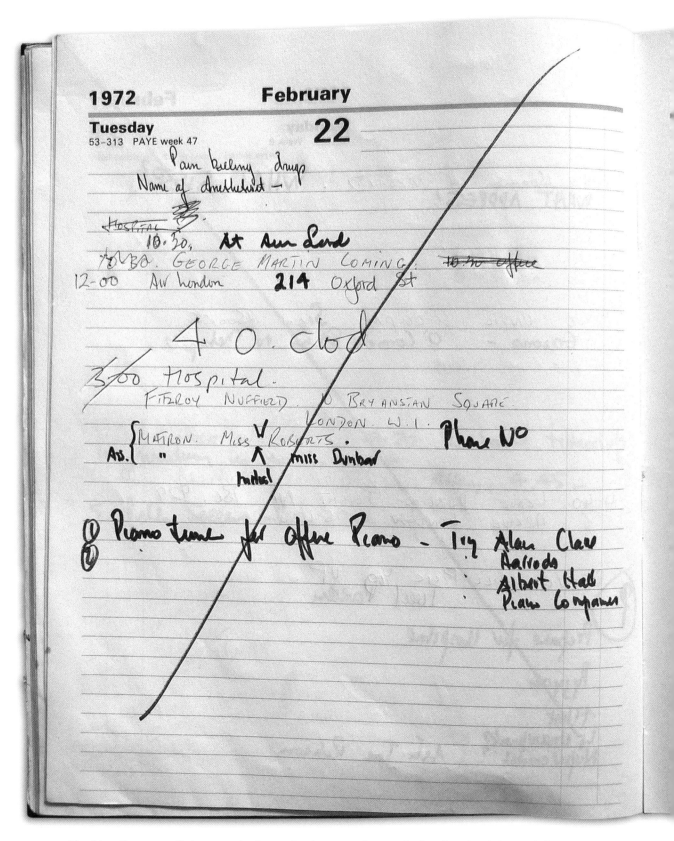

Tuesday   **22**
53–313   PAYE week 47

Pain killing drugs
Name of Anethetist —

Hospital
10.30,   At Sun Lord
NBA. GEORGE MARTIN COMING.   10.30 office
12·00   AW London   **214** Oxford St

4 O. clock

3/00   Hospital.
FITZROY NUFFIELD   10 BRYANSTAN SQUARE.
LONDON. W. 1.   Phone No
Matron. Miss ⱽ Roberts.
Ass. ["   ᴧ   miss Dunbar
              Initial

Promo tune for Office Piano — Try Alan Clau
                                                   Harrods
                                                   Albert Hall
                                                   Piano Companies

Checking the name of the anaesthetist so that he can make sure he is using the right painkillers.

Wednesday
54–312
Ember Day

23

Sun Flower Seed

HOSPITAL

7.15 Operation   SURGEON. MR. E.E. O'MALLEY.

Good luck - Spike Milligan

Making sure he has his sunflower seeds and wishing himself good luck – I loved that.

Padby said she will pick one up before 11 o'clock the wall phone and when she's coming.

1972 **March**

Friday
63—303

3

Start to write   Aquarius

(1) Is Milligan for all Seasons on — write and ask.

(2) Whats with 'Adolph Film?

(3)

Go home from hospital — Operation not so bad — I'm glad I over came my fear of this particular operation — it was one I knew was terribly painful well — it wasn't so bad. Its still very sore and bleeds but I'm to see the Doc in a weeks time.

The operation was for haemorrhoids and Spike had been told it would be very painful. He refused any food – hence the sunflower seeds – and Matron Roberts was driven mad by him. He told her he wouldn't eat solids and 'crap broken glass to please you'. He lived on jelly and sunflower seeds instead.

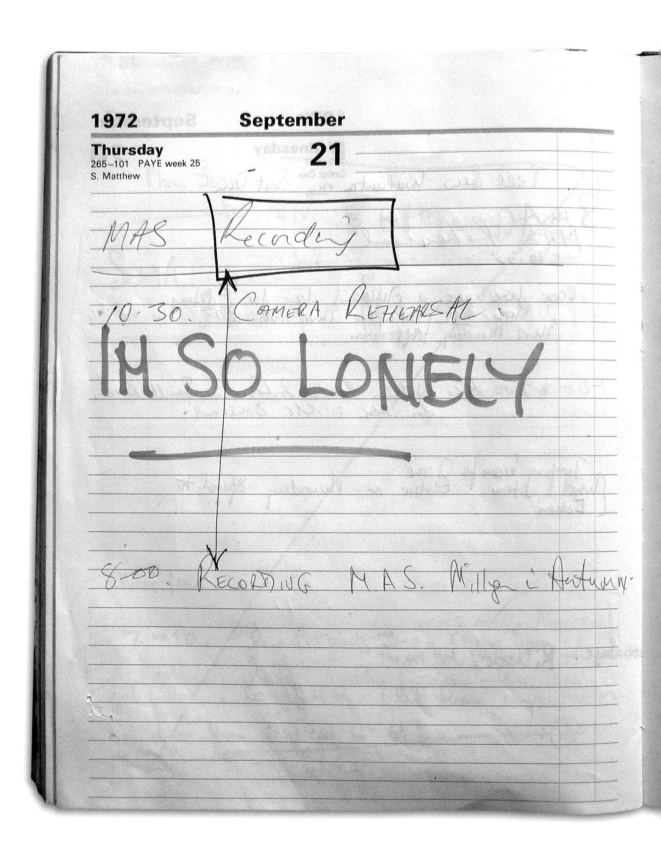

This was always the feeling he would get before going into a depression. It never changed.

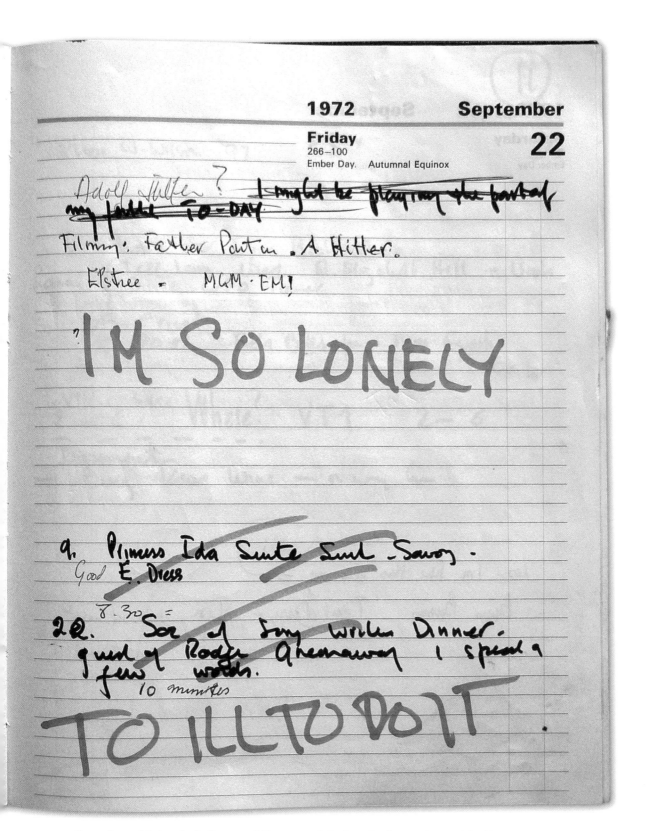

Friday   **22**
266–100
Ember Day. Autumnal Equinox

Adolf Hitler ? ~~I might be playing the part of~~
~~my father~~ TO-DAY

Filming: Father Painter. A Hitler.

Elstree —   MGM · EMI

'IM SO LONELY

9. Princess Ida Suite Suml - Savoy.
    Good E. Dress

22. 8.30 =
     Sat et Sony Writers Dinner.
     guest of Roger Greenaway I speak a
     few words.
          10 minutes

TO ILL TO DO IT .

Sometimes this lonely feeling would last a week before the depression took hold. On this occasion it took only one day.

? Op on hand.   Ⓝ Same hospital - same room please

① Water in Well.
② Key to 127 : Holden Rd
③ Carpenter
④ _____

What room at hospital
Look at TV Show - file extra material - ✓
① Chinese - Sentry!
② Collect material to chose from for S.w Winde ✓
③ Kids fairy stories.   Being typed
④ Where is hand written fairy story
⑤ Consider One Man Show. Try it on a few
    Sunday Charity Concerts - ~~Sandy Brown~~ Singer.
⑥ ~~Sam~~ J. Franz - Waltz in C   Get Tape Copy X
⑦ Waltz in C. Palm Court .   Get Tape Copy X
⑧ Press, op on hand - Wrote message on left on
    " ~~This way to the operating~~ Doc. he on escommand as poss!
⑩ I've had a bad year".   M. Came.
⑪ Lawn Mowers
    Shelves.
12 Ombudsman - re official received
6 Oc   Fitzroy Nuffield   ~~Head~~-
            Bryanston ☐ ?
                Mrs Roberts
        Dr. Evans . 828 - 3038 office
                    946 - 4016

Idea" Answering machine :   Quarter an inch
        "This is an answer. your dinner is in the Oven

~~Fred~~ Paddy came - She will bring Sile & Jane Tomorrow after School

~~GOOD OLD DAYS B.B.C. LEEDS.~~

- There was a little fly -

Nov 27
In abhorent memory of Colonel Geo Armstrong Custer
US Cavalry who on this day in 1868 · massacred
without warning the ~~red~~ village of Chief Black Kettle and
his Cheyennes, men- women and children.

Mermaid. — Mummmys Show
& Show. — ?

What on earth brought this on?

P Speak Paddy wed end
Tickets for Sean

Mums Birthday ←|

RECORDING MILLIGAN IN WINTER

The first Noel
It caused ruddn hell
People all asleep
Was a cow

Good King Wenceslas looked out
On the feast of Steven Steven
He'd left his car on a yellow line
And
Then there came a warden who
Stuck upon a windscreen
Two pound ten to pay

RECORDING MILLIGAN IN WINTER.

First ideas. He would then either hone them before the show or 'bin them'.

Ask (P) if I'm Free for tonight

{ Tell Norma Slogitt again.

Xmas Presents.

(1) (N) Aumteon for home lashd (N) what bill — $50,000
(N) When is next meeting of Pen Working
Steering Committee.
(2) Write re Post War Credits
(3) BUPA Write - to Managing Director or $40 — £100
(4) Wrap my presents
Buy Wines To-mon

Fungacid • 743-1272

Bill Martin 1 X 6562
8712

Aftern... meet Clyde medal, Sellers me
No point if Sellers isn't there.

{ Whitechapel Art Gallery. Tdd P. I don't know what
Afternn time

5-00. NATIONWIDE LIME GROVE T.V
GOON PRESERVATION SOCIETY.

(P)

{ Tell Paddy Paddy Cant come

X { J. Hobbs. dinner Trafoo } X
Wines

X

Getting himself organised for Christmas. He really did wrap his presents every year. Mind you, he had to remind himself.

35

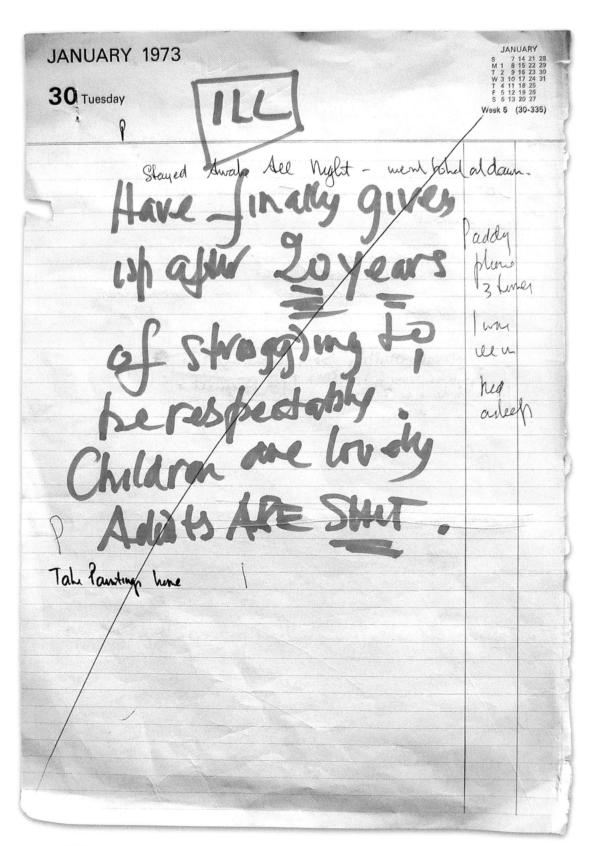

JANUARY 1973

30 Tuesday

ILL

JANUARY
S   7 14 21 28
M 1 8 15 22 29
T 2 9 16 23 30
W 3 10 17 24 31
T 4 11 18 25
F 5 12 19 26
S 6 13 20 27
Week 5   (30-335)

Stayed Awake All Night — went bohd at dawn.

Have finally given
up after 20 years
of struggling to
be respectably
Children are lovely
Adults ARE SHIT.

Paddy
phone
3 times

I was
seen
had
asleep

Take Paintings home

Pure Milligan.

NOVEMBER
S   4 11 18 25
M 5 12 19 26
T 6 13 20 27
W 7 14 21 28
T 1 8 15 22 29
F 2 9 16 23 30
S 3 10 17 24
(295-70) Week 43

1973 OCTOBER

Monday **22**

Spike

Scenes . 84 . 85   112 – 113.
Rough Weather Alternative 192, 193 A 194
G. N.

McGonigal the 'Bill.'
    Ted Sturgess

— ALL DAY AT SEA —

Pete Sellers gulfed up – left the ship
went back to his tin Villa –
Gloom every where – I tried to re-jig the
shoot, but no one listened

Conference with P-Medach

Lette from Paddy – fine
of fever fell ill –
went to bed – B. 3.

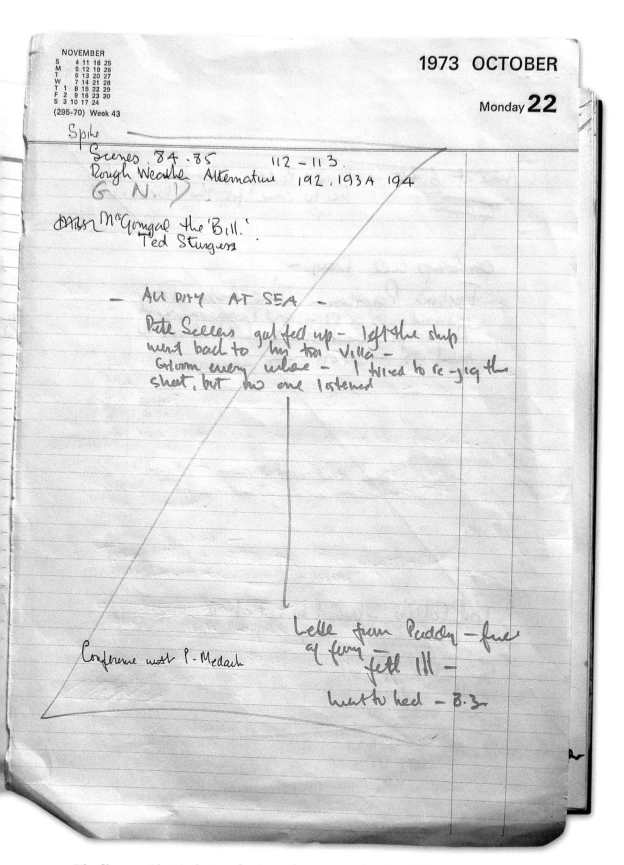

The film was *Ghost in the Noonday Sun* and we were on location in Kyrenia.

OCTOBER 1973

23 Tuesday

OCTOBER
S   7 14 21 28
M 1 8 15 22 29
T 2 9 16 23 30
W 3 10 17 24 31
T 4 11 18 25
F 5 12 19 26
S 6 13 20 27

Week 43 (296-69)

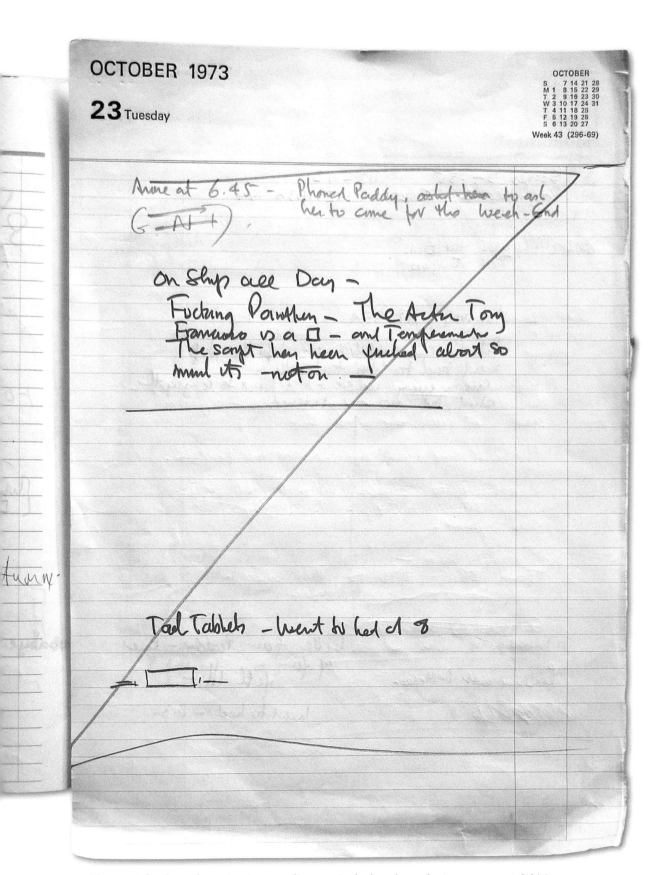

Arose at 6.45 — Phoned Paddy, asked her to ask
her to come for the week-End
(G.A.T)

On Ship all Day —
Fucking Panthea — The Actor Tony
Francioso is a ☐ — and Temperamen
The Script has been fucked about so
much its — not on. —

Dad Tablets — Went to bed at 8

— ☐ —

He was right about the script: it was a disaster. And what about the 'temperamental' bit!

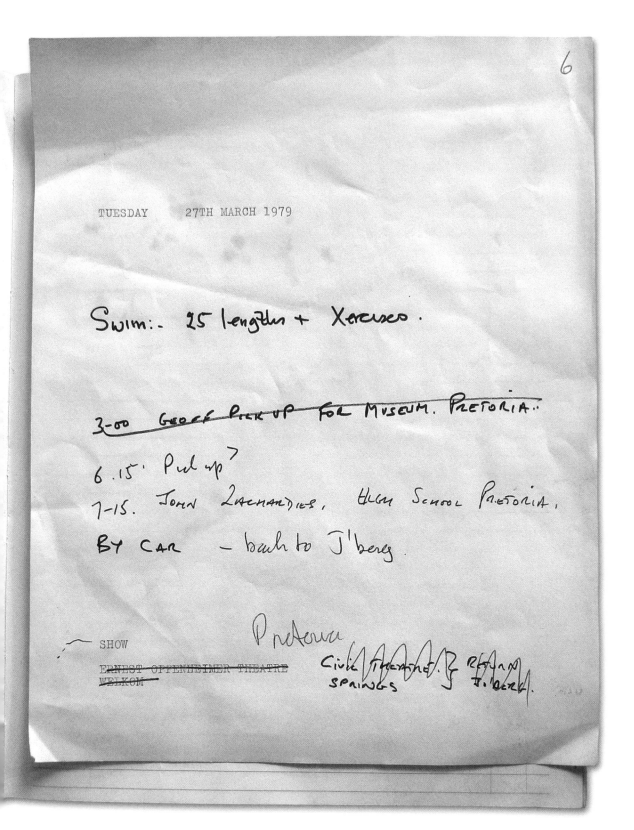

TUESDAY   27TH MARCH 1979

Swim:- 25 lengths + Xercises.

3-00 Geoff Pick up for Museum. Pretoria.

6.15. Pick up?
7-15. John Zachardies, High School Pretoria,
By Car   — back to J'berg.

SHOW

~ ERNEST OPPENHEIMER THEATRE
WELKOM

Pretoria

Civic Theatre.   R
SPRINGS   J.'berg

On tour in South Africa, Spike maintained his fitness regime, even in the heat. One day he swam 100 lengths of the pool. Had I not witnessed it I would never have believed him, and would have put it down to one of his fantasies.

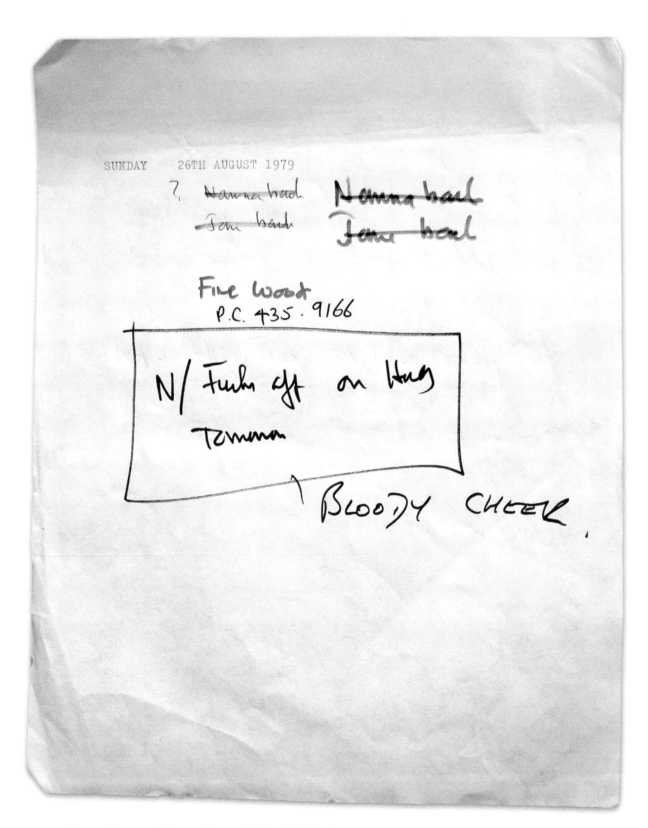

SUNDAY   26TH AUGUST 1979

Me earning a well-deserved rest. Obviously Spike doesn't agree. My comments made him laugh.

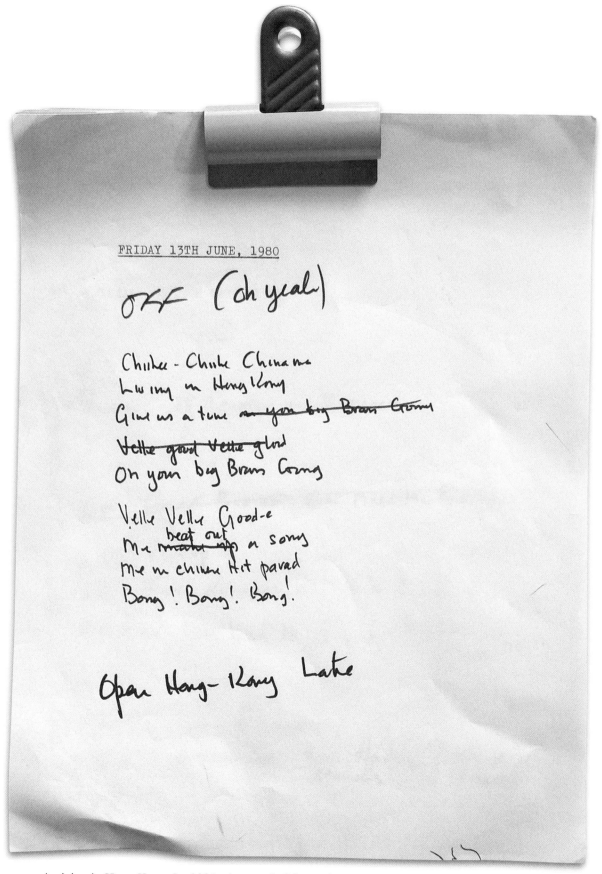

FRIDAY 13TH JUNE, 1980

OKF (oh yeah)

Chikee - Chikee Chinamie
Living in Hong Kong
Give us a tune ~~on your big Brass Gong~~

~~Vette good vette glod~~
On your big Brass Gong

Vette Velle Good-e
Me ~~made up~~ beat out a song
Me in chinee Hit parad
Bong! Bong! Bong!

Open Hong-Kong Lake

Arriving in Hong Kong, I told him it was a holiday and I wrote it in his diary. A poem on his arrival – something for Box 18.

41

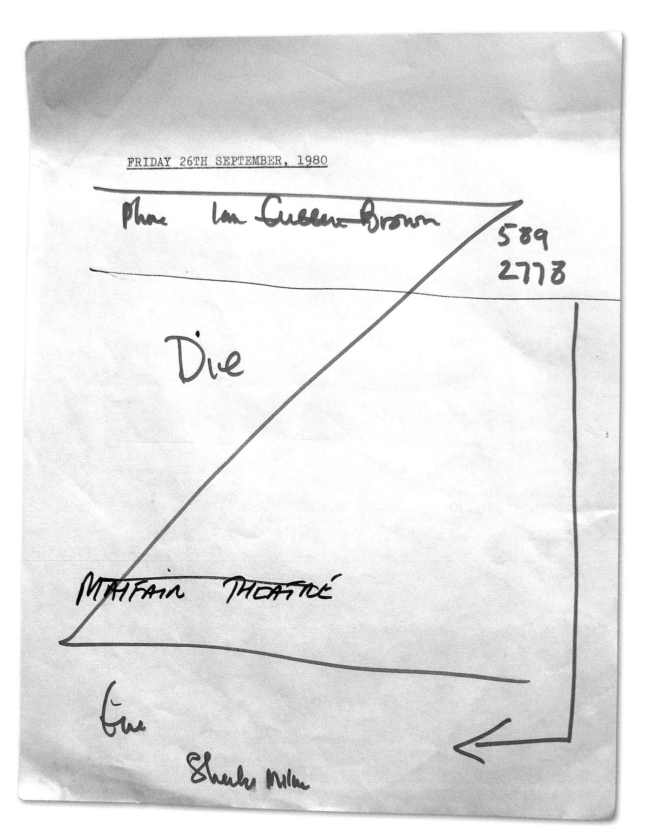

He didn't.

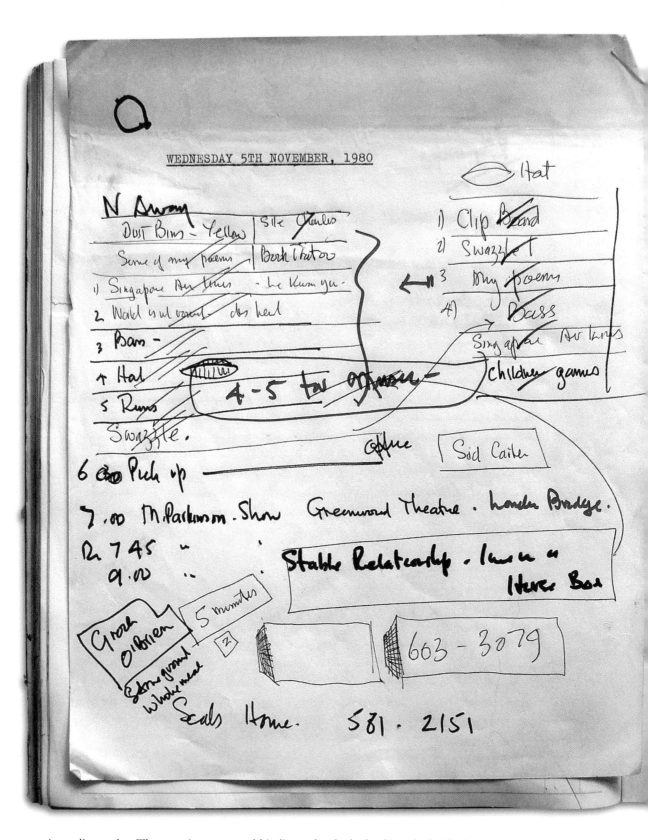

An ordinary day. The crossing-out would indicate that he had achieved what he had set out to do.

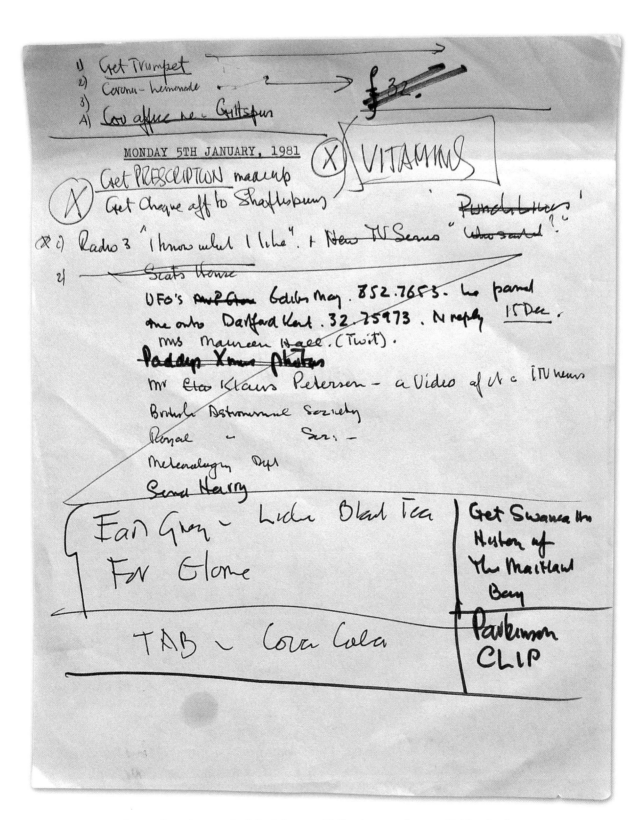

Another ordinary day – but not for Mrs Maureen Hall, whoever she was. Evidently she was someone who didn't have the information he wanted at that time.

SCRIPTS FOR MILLIGAN'S MILLENNIUM

DUMMY SKETCH

Front room middle class. On the couch is a terrible dummy of a middle aged man. The son is seated on a chair. The mother is knitting.

Son: Mum, Mum.

Mother: Oh what is it now – you've made me drop a stitch.

Son: Mum why did you marry a dummy?

Mother: Lots of reasons, one, he can't answer back, two, if I go and hit him **(she crosses and hits him)** he doesn't complain.

Son: But you can't have children – .

Mother: I had you.

Son: Er – how mother?

Mother: A sperm donor.

Son: You mean my father was a sperm donor.

Mother: One of them.

Son: Which one?

Mother: One called Fred.

Son: Oh, my father was Fred, what was his family name?

Mother: Zakenthrusterbergensteiner Company Limited.

Son: My dad had a limited company?

Mother: Very limited, there was only me.

Son: Is he still alive?

Mother: No.

Son: Is he dead?

Mother: Well they buried him.

Son: Answer the question!

Milligan's Millennium was going to be a TV show produced by my dear friend John Fisher. It never got off the ground, but remained in Box 18.

Dummy Sketch

Front Room middle class. On the couch is a terrible dummy of a middle aged man

The son is seated on a chair.

The mother is knitting.

Son   Mum. Mum.

Mother   Oh what is it I know - you've me drop a stich

Son   Mum why did you marry a dummy?

Mother   Lots of reasons, one, he can't answer back two, if I go too far but him (she crosses and hits him) he doesn't complain.

Son   But you can't have children -

Mother: I had you.

Son   Er - _how_ mother

Mother   a sperm doner

Son   You mean my father was a sperm done

Mother   One of them.

Son   Which one -

Mother   One called Fred

Son   Oh, my father was fred, what was his family name

Mother   Zakenthrusterbergsteiner * Company limited

Son   Why did had limited Company?

mother   Very limited. there was only me

Son   Is he still alive?

Mothe   Hes dead

mothe   no

Son   Is he dead

mother   well they buried him

Son   Answer the Quetic!

mother   Looks at Camera (fade)

47

Sentry on Duty.   Officer approaches.

Officer: 'Good evening, sentry.'

Sentry: 'Good evening, sir.'

Officer: 'Look, don't you salute an officer?'

Sentry: 'No sir.'

Officer: 'Why not?'

Sentry: 'It's my religion.   I'm a Catholic - Catholics
               don't salute officers.'

Officer: 'Who said so?'

Sentry: 'The Pope.'

Officer: 'The Pope?   He has no authority to stop you
               saluting officers.'

Sentry: 'Oh yes he has, sir.'

Officer: 'Who from?'

Sentry: 'God sir, you mustn't disobey God, sir.'

Officer   'Where does it say that?'

Sentry: 'In the Book of Genesis, 'The Lord sayeth that
               soldiers don't have to salute officers.'

Officer: 'Show me the book.' Sentry hands him the book,
               officer turns thru the pages.   'It doesn't say
               it in this book.'

Sentry   'It does, there.' Points to book.

Officer: 'It says "and Abraham sacrificed a ram.'

Sentry: 'Yes, and that translated into Hebrew means you
               don't have to salute an officer.'

Elephant Substitute

Newspaper Headlines (with dramatic music)

LONDON ZOO RUNS OUT OF ELEPHANTS!
[Search for alternatives]

Cage in zoo. Man with an elephant trunk attached to face.
Visitor, clutching a dummy of a school boy. Speaks to attendant.

Visitor: 'That's not a real elephant.'

Attendant: 'No sir, that's an elephant substitute.'

Visitor: 'You must be joking.'

Attendant: 'No sir, that is a genuine elephant substitute.'

Visitor: 'But I brought my son here to see a real
                elephant.'

Attendant: 'Is that your son?'

Visitor: 'Yes.'

Attendant: 'Why is he all floppy?'

Visitor: 'He's not a real son, he's a son substitute.

Attendant: [To camera] 'It's a strange world.'

Troonaphant

49

Australian Sketch

London street, into it leaps an Australian (hat with corks), he bounds like a kangaroo. He has a ball and chain round his ankle and wears convict's suit.   'I claim this land fer Orstralia?' He sings

Orstralia - Orstralia

We think of you each day

Orstralia - Orstralia

At work or at play

We think of yew in the morning

And in the evening too

We even wake up at mid-night

So that we can think of you.

Orstralia - Orstralia

We love you from the heart

the kidneys, the liver and the giblets

And every other part.

Policeman: ''ello, 'ello, 'ello, wot are you a doin' of?'

Australian: 'I've just claimed this land as Australia.'

Policeman: 'Then you must have maken a mistake, sir. This place is called England!'

Burst of 'Land of Hope and Glory', police salutes stands to attention.'

Australian: 'England, that's where the Poms come from.'

Policeman: 'Yes.'

Australian: 'Are you a bloody Pom?'

Policeman: 'Yes, I'm a bloody Pom policeman.'

Australian: 'Listen, Rolph Harris lives here, this must be Orstralia.'

Policeman: 'Look, if you don't believe me, I'll take you to see the Queen of England.'

A living room of a working class family. Against one wall the throne of England, on it sits a thirty year old working class frump, wearing the Crown of England.

Policeman pushes door into set. Knocks, a liveried footman answers the door.

Policeman: 'Is the Queen in?'

Footman: 'Yes, she's on the throne at the moment.'

Policeman and Australian go in. There sits a middle class woman in a front room with a throne against the wall.

Policeman: 'Her Majesty, the Queen.' Salutes.

Burst of 'Land of Hope and Glory.' Policeman stands to attention.

Australian: 'Christ, surely you can do better than that'

Policeman: 'Look, she's only a working class Queen. The real Queen lives in Buckingham Palace, but she would meet the likes of you.'

Australian: 'The Bum to the Queen of England' (TO CAMERA)

Footman: 'Ladies and gentlemen, because this man has insulted the Queen, this sketch must end.

Elephant

Line of WC's   all vacant except one

Man tries to open door

2man:. Thats in use – its an elephant

man   Elephant? Wots he doing in there

2man   Having a crap
            ^ Elephant?)
man   ^ He'll smash the, seat   blot?

2man   Yes. I heard that go – whe
            not me ^one the others?.

A

Man   No I've left my watch in than this one.

2man   Well I can tell you the time its one-twenty
            Hes been in there an hour and a half

Man   Well Suppose and Elephant do does a lot shit. to do

2man   I'll try and hurry up in there (knocks on door) Hurry
            up in there

          Sound of elephant. trumpeting

Man look: Ive got an appointment – I'll only be 20 min
            Could you retrieve my watch

Man2   Of course

Caption 20 minutes later

Same W.C.s the elephant cubicle is empty
Man returns. Ah! did you get my watch
Man2 No – he was wearing it.

Exterior Zoo Whipsnade
Ticket office. Ticket man
Man enters: Excuse me one of your elephants is
            wearing my watch
TM oh Would you recognise the elephant
Man   Oh Yes. he'll wearing a watch.
            (To camera) t Think that as far as you
            can go in this sketch)

52

ELEPHANT

Line of WC's all vacant except one.
Man tries to open door

2 Man: That's in use – its an elephant.

Man: Elephant? wots he doing in there

2 Man: Having a crap.

Man: Elephant? He'll smash the bloody seat.

2 Man: Yes I heard that go – why not use one of the others?

Man: No I've left my watch in this one.

2 Man: Well I can tell you the time its one-twenty. He's been in there an hour and a half.

Man: Well I suppose an elephant has a lot to do.

2 Man: I'll try and hurry him up in there **(knocks on door)** Hurry up in there.

Sound of elephant trumpeting

Man: Look I've got an appointment. I'll only be 20 minutes. Could you retrieve my watch?

2 Man: Of course.

Caption 20 minutes later
Same WC's – the elephant cubicle is empty.

Man returns: Ah did you get my watch?

2 Man: No- he was wearing it.

Exterior Zoo Whipsnade
Ticket office. Ticket man

Man enters: Excuse me one of your elephants is wearing my watch

TM: Oh would you recognise the elephant

Man: Oh yes, he'll be wearing a watch
(**to camera** – I think this is as far as you can go in this sketch)

1958: First trip to Australia to appear on ABC Sydney. The show was called *Idiots' Weekly*.

Hitler Job

Job Exchange. Queue. 2nd man in queue is Hitler.

Clerk: 'Hello, I've never seen you here before.'

Hitler: 'No, zis is meine first time.'

Clerk: 'Name?'

Hitler: 'O'Brien, I'm O'Brien.'

Clerk: [Long look]. No you're not. You're Adolph
            Hitler.'

Hitler: 'Yes.'

Clerk: 'I thought you were dead. It said you blew your
            brains out in a cellar.'

Hitler: 'Ya, but I missed.'

Clerk: 'Well what are you doin' 'ere?'

Hitler: 'I'm looking for a job.'

Clerk: 'Oh? Wot you want, bricklayer, plumber?

Hitler: 'No, meine old job was Dictator.

Clerk: 'Well we ain't got any vacancies for dictators.
            I'll put your name down and if one turns up we'll
            phone. Have you got British citizenship?'

Hitler: 'Listen [sings].

                 Gott save our gracious Queen,

                 Long live our noble Queen

                 Gott save our Queen. Sieg Heil!!'

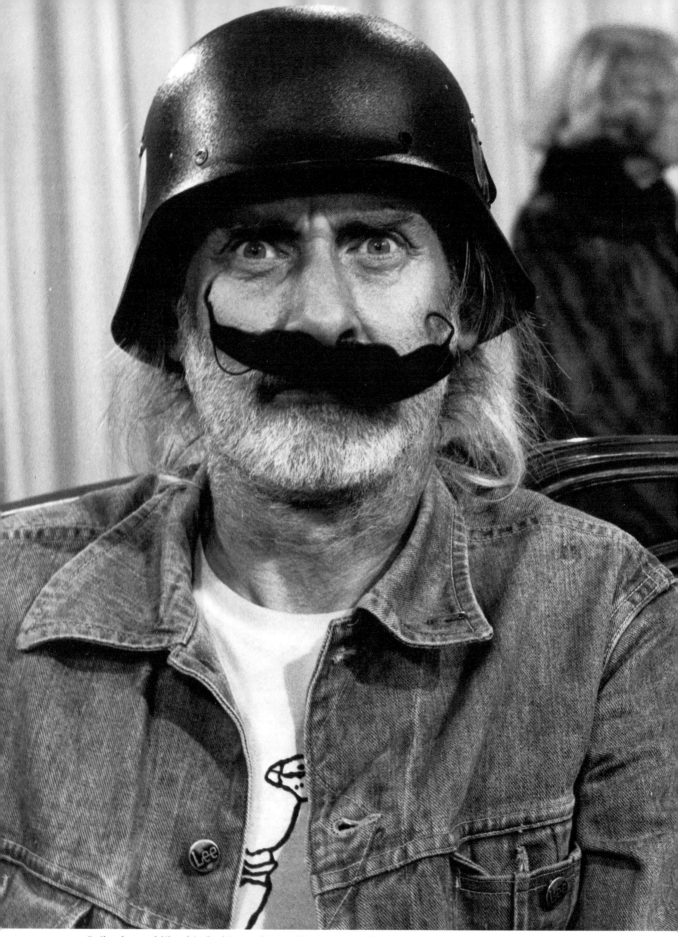

Spike dressed like this for his mother's *This Is Your Life*. There's nothing more to say.

BIBLE SKETCH

Woman dressed as Virgin Mary, comes out of office door

V.Mary: He'll see you now Peter

Interview at Office, behind desk sits Jesus Christ (Chis Langham)
Enter Peter (Spike)

Peter: You wanted to see me Jesus

Jesus: Yes Peter, pull up a chair.

Peter: I'd rather stand.

Jesus: Alright stand on a chair.

Peter: What's this all about Jesus?

Jesus: Peter, listen, when the cock crows three times you will deny me.

Peter: On no I won't

Jesus: Oh yes you will.

Standing by Jesus is a Roman soldier

Roman: Do you know this man?

Peter: No I deny it

This is Good.

Cut to grotty stuffed duck

V: Quack Quack

Peter: That wasn't a cock!

Roman: Do you know this man?

Peter: No I deny it.

Cut to grotty stuffed parrot

V: Pretty polly – pretty polly

Parrot gets hit with a mallet

Me giving Spike my approval – as though he would take any notice.

Bible Sketch, continued:

Peter: That wasn't a cock! Jesus

Roman: Do you know this man

Peter: No I deny it.

Cut to grotty stuffed dog

V: Woof-woof-woof **hit with mallet**

Peter: And **that** wasn't a cock. Jesus.

Jesus: I'm sorry Peter I've been let down by the effects department **(break down)**

Football Referee blows whistle

F.R: Half-time

2-3 minutes

Goon bird

Bible Sketch

Woman dressed as Virgin Mary, comes out of office door

V Mary: He'll see you now Peter

Interior of Office, behind desk sits Jesus Christ (Chris Langham)

Enter Peter (Spike) You wanted to see me Jesus

Jesus Yes peter, pull up a chair

Peter I'd rather stand

Jesus Alright stand on a chair

Peter Wats this all about Jesus.

Jesus Peter, listen, when the cock crows three times you
will deny me.

Peter Oh no I wont

Jesus Oh yes you will.

Standing by Jesus is a Roman soldier

Roman Do you know this man

Peter No I deny it

Cut to grotty stuffed duck

V. Quack- Quack.

Peter that was'nt a cock! cock.

Roman Do Do you know this man?

Peter No I deny it.

Cut to Grotty stuffed parrot

V Pretty Polly - pretty polly.

Parrot gets hit with a mallet

Peter that was'nt a cock! Jesus.

Roman Do you know this man

Peter No - I denyed deny it.

Cut to grotty stuffed dog

Woof - Woof - Woof Hit with mallet

Peter And that was'nt a cock Jesus

(Grauho Mark. Don't believe all you)
read in the Bible.

Jesus I'm sorry Peter I've
been let down by the effects department
(breaks down)

Football referee, blows whistle
'F.R.' Half-time   2-3 mins

⟨S⟩ THIS IS GOOD)
YOU CAN OPEN ON THIS

My way of trying to encourage him.

60

Virgin Mary comes out door: 'Alright you can go in now, Peter.'
Peter goes in. Jesus is sitting behind desk. A man stands behind him.

Peter: 'You wanted to see me, Jesus?'

Jesus: 'Yes Peter, when the cock crows three times you will deny it.'

Peter: 'Oh no I won't.'

Jesus: 'Oh yes you will.'

Grotty parrot squawks three times.

Man points to Jesus: 'Do you know this man?'

Peter: 'No.'

Jesus: 'You see?'

Peter: 'That wasn't a cock, it was a parrot.'

Jesus: 'Oh no it wasn't.'

Peter: 'Oh yes it was.'

Jesus: 'When the cock crows three times you will deny me.'

Grotty parrot squawks three times.

Man to Peter: 'Do you know this man?'

Peter: 'No. I deny it.'

Soldier Sketch

Soldier: 'I am a soldier, I shoot people. Ah, there's one
               now. Bang!'

Man: 'Oh oh oh oh - ow owo Oh-oh ah.'

Soldier: 'This man is going for the over acting award of
               the year.'

Policeman: 'ello, 'ello, 'ello, wot's a goin on 'ere?' I be
               of assistance?   A mouth to mouth, or heart
               resuscitation?'

Man: 'That man has just killed me.'

Policeman: 'That is a very serious charge.   Have you any
               evidence of the occurrence?'

Man: 'Yes, this, my death certificate.'

Policeman: 'This will come in very useful at the enquiry.

   In Court.

Judge: 'The victim appears to be proper dead alive.'

Solicitor: 'Yes, my client is waiting for the case to end to
               be proper dead[?]'

Judge: 'You - you killed this man, do you plead guilty,
               or not guilty?'

Man: 'Oh, I've got a choice, I'll go for not guilty.'

Judge: 'Go, I get home early for dinner - we got
               spaghetti rings tonight.'

Cat - Coffin

Front door.

RSPCA man knocks.

Door opens by a housewife.

Housewife: 'Yes?'

RSPCA: 'Good morning madam, I'm from the RSPCA. I've come to make arrangements in the event of your cat dying.'

Woman: 'Oh, what do you want to do?'

RSPCA: 'Measure him for a cat - coffin.'

Woman: 'It's a strange request - but come in.'

RSPCA man comes in with three different-sized small cat - coffins. Picks up a floppy stuffed cat.

RSPCA: 'Can I just try your cat on one?' (Picks up cat, tries it in the box). 'Perfect! Do you want the cat tail included?'

Woman: 'You're not going to cut it off are you?'

RSPCA: 'Oh no madam - but the tail will need an extension to the box (puts extension for tail to coffin). 'Perfect. Now would you like to pay for it in advance?'

Woman: 'No, he isn't dead yet.'

RSPCA: 'Well you don't want to wait til the last moment.'

Woman: 'Yes I do. Actually I'm waiting for the last moment.'

Two Egyptologists with torches walking in an underground tomb.
Suddenly they come upon a casket with Egyptian hieroglyphics.
1st Egyptian: 'My God, Sanders, this is it?' (He reads
hieroglyphics). "Here lies the body of Im-oth-the II Pharoah of
all Egypt." Carefully they lift the lid, then gasp.
1st Egyptian: We're too late - he's dead!'

Corny chord from Orchestra.

The Cliffs. Brighton

[V.O.] Man standing at cliff edge enjoying the view¬

Caption: Man Standing on the Cliffs, Brighton enjoying the view.

2nd Man   'Excuse me interrupting, are you going to be standing
           here long?'

1st Man   'No, why?'

2nd Man   'My mother-in-law wants to commit suicide from here.'

1st Man   'Oh, didn't you try to stop her?'

2nd Man   'No, in fact it was I who suggested it.'

1st Man   'Why does she want to commit suicide?'

2nd Man   'Because I suggested it.'

1st Man   'Is she going to jump?'

2nd Man   'No, she's taking aspirin.'

1st Man   'That won't kill her.'

2nd Man   'She's taking ten thousand.'

Optican

So   Man comes into Opticans shop

Optican.   Yes sir what can I do for you

.Man   Can I see an Optican

Optican   Not with out glass sir

Man   You se I - I- can't see

Optican   Thats why you can't see em optican

Man   I can't see at all

Optican   Oh- come out side sir | OUTSIDE |

Outside Hand holds out sign

Optican   Now sir look up

Man   Do I have too

Optican   Yes

(man looks up)

Optican   Can you see the sun

Man   Yes.

Optican   How bloody far do you want to see

Man   I only want to see as Far as Doris Watson

Optican   Why

Man   Shes got big boobs.

~~Optican Oh~~
~~Man   If not I want to see her mother Rita~~

~~Optican   Why~~
~~Man   She got bigger boobs~~

Optican   I sorry we don't have that type of glasses

Man   What type have you got

Optican   These (Hands him two pint glasses)

Man   Holds them up like binoculars

Optican   Can you see anything

Man   Yes I can see you - but you have'nt
got big boobs.

OPTICIAN

Man comes into optician's shop

Optician: Yes sir what can I do for you?

Man: Can I see an optician?

Optician: Not without glasses sir.

Man: You see I-I- can't see.

Optician: That's why you can't see an optician.

Man: I can't see at all.

Optician: Oh- come outside sir.

Hand holds out sign OUTSIDE

Optician: Now sir look up.

Man: Do I have to.

Optician: Yes

(Man looks up)

Optician: Can you see the sun?

Man: Yes

Optician: How bloody far do you want to see?

Man: I only want to see as far as Doris Watson

Optician: Why

Man: She's got big boobs.

Optician: I'm sorry we don't have that type of glasses.

Man: What type have you got?

Optician: These **(hands him two pint glasses)**.

Man holds them up like binoculars

Optician: Can you see anything?

Optician sketch, continued

Man: Yes I can see you – but you haven't got big boobs

Optician: Sorry

Milligan Preserved LP. Spike, John Antrobus, Valentine Dyall and Paddy Milligan.

Around 1945 or 1946: A rare photo of the Bill Hall Trio. Alexander Club, Rome. The start of it all.

HERMAN GORING

Herman Goring found himself driving a NO.112A bus to Catford. Wot in Gods name am I doing driving a NO.112A bus to Catford, No I should be broadcasting Nazi propaganda on Radio Berlin. A British Bobby halted the bus. he approach the driving cab and said ' Herman Goring I arrest you for been a Nazi, and a danger to the Royal Family' " How can I harm zer Royal Family, zey have Iron railing around the Palace, and a Sentry on guard with a bearskin and a loaded rifle... ' I must ask you to come down to the Station. Meekly Goring obeyed. and ended up in a cell 12 foot by ten, with another prisoner who was drunk and being sick. 'This is an insult to me' he shouted thru the bars, I'm used to sumptious living, in the grand manner³ᵉʳ " " Well fuck you luck" said a Police Sergeant' Handing him a plate of beans and porridge " I can't eat zis crap' he said ' You dont have too' said the Bobby' You can keep it" ' I'll keep it in zer fridge' said Goring ' It vill keep longer". The fridge was broken, the whole meal came out covered in mildew, but Goring was hungry he ate the meal mildew and all, but an hour later, he started to go green, a Green Goring was something to behold, he hid this by spraying him flesh pink, he stood out in a crowd... he even stood out on his own

Fuck zis for a life' he swore.
"You know Herman' said his wife'
' I find you most attractive in pink"
Good this promises some extra fucks

Please, no letters telling me this has been published before. I can't find it – so, OK, it definitely hasn't been published in Spike's handwriting before. 10/10, Norma.

HERMAN GORING found himself driving a No 112A bus to Catford.

Wot in Gods name am I doing driving a No 112A bus to Catford, No I should be broadcasting Nazi propaganda on Radio Berlin.

A British Bobby halted the bus. he approach the driving cab and said 'Herman Goring I arrest you for been a Nazi, and a danger to the Royal Family'

'How can I harm zer Royal Family, zey have iron railing around the Palace, and a Sentry on guard with a bearskin and a loaded rifle.

'I must ask you to come down to the Station. Meekly Goring obeyed, and ended up in a cell 12 foot by ten, with another prisoner who was drunk and being sick.

'This is an insult to me' he shouted thru the bars, I'm used to sumptuous living, in zer grand manner'

'Well, fuck you luck' said a Police Sergeant Handing him a plate of beans and porridge

'I can't eat zis crap' he said

'You don't have too' said the Bobby 'You can keep it.'

'I'll keep it in zer fridge' said Goring 'It vill keep longer.'

The fridge was broken, the whole meal came out covered in mildew, but Goring was hungry he ate the meal mildew and all, but an hour later, he started to go green, a Green Goring was something to behold, he hid this by spraying him flesh pink, he stood out in a crowd . . . he even stood out on his own

Fuck zis for a life' he swore.

'You know Herman' said his wife 'I find you most attractive in pink'

Good this promises some extra fucks

Meantime on the farm Hitler was feeding the pigs 'Jewish swine' he bellowed at them. The pigs were not moved. 'You all look like the swine Churchill. I'll make him pay for zis war.'

Churchill had no intention in paying for the war. At that moment Churchill was tucking into roast phesant and chips while drinking a vintage Burgundy I wonder what that Nazee bastard is doing. I would think that at this time of night he would be thinking of screwing Eva Braun, said his man servant.

'I hope she gives him a dose' growled the great man, pouring himself some rare old brandy 'Couldn't win the war with a this stuff.'

We certainly could all do with a good stuff' said his man servant.

'Tell my secretary Miss Dobson, to prepare for one.'

An hour later Churchill lifted himself off Miss Dobson pouring with sweat. 'How much will that be Miss Dobson.'

As it was in my free time, a hundred and ten pounds.

He wrote out a cheque for the amount. 'Just give me time to get out of the country'

Cheque was returned 'Insufficient funds'.

Bugger said Miss Dobson 'I've been fucked for nothing' To cover himself he gave her an IOU. 'When will this become due' said Miss Dobson.

'Christmas,' said Churchill.

'Christmas?' said Miss Dobson. 'That ten <u>bloody months</u> away.'

'So it is' said Churchill

'I can't wait that long' said Miss Dobson.

'Well, I <u>can</u>,' said Churchill and buggered off. He went to ten Downing Street as he live there rent free. Churchill was short of money all of his life, and even after that

'Darling, you must stop buying black silk underwear' said Clementine.

'Why' said Churchill 'no one can see them'!

'They're too expensive dear.'

'Look' said Churchill 'I'm Prime Minister of England, if I can't afford it, who can? eh? eh?'

'But at the end of the month we're broke' said Clementine.

'Oh, I've been in tighter spots than that' he laughed.

'Well were overdrawn at the bank by ten thousand pounds'

'Well, I've been in tighter spots than <u>that</u>' he said lighting a Havana Cigar and sipping a brandy. 'Lord Beaverbrook is going to give me ten thousand pounds for writing an article on life in the Artic' he said.

'Youve never been to the Artic' said Clementine

'Ah but he does'nt know that, said Churchill

'That's cheating' said Clementine stamping her foot, and breaking her ankle 'Now look what you've made me do' she said limping away.

Meantime on the farm Hitler was feeding the pigs 'Jewish swine' he bellowed at them. The pigs were not moved. 'You all look like the swine Churchill. ~~Churchill~~. I'll make him pay for zis war.' Churchill had no intention in paying for the war. At that moment Churchill was tucking into roast phesant and ~~clapp~~ chips while drinking a vintage Burgundy 'I wonder what that Nazee bastard is doing. I would think that at this time of night he would be thinking of screwing Eva Braun,' said his man servant. 'I hope she gives him a dose.' growled the great man. pouring himself some rare old brandy 'Couldn't win the war with a this stuff.' We certainly could all do with a good stuff said his man servant. 'Tell my secretary Mrs Dobson, to prepare for one.' An hour later Churchill lifted off himself Mrs Dobson pouring with sweat. 'How much will that be Mrs Dobson. As it was in my free time, a hundred and ten pounds. He wrote out a cheque for the amount. 'Just give me time to get out of the countri' Cheque was redeemed 'In sufficent funds' Bugger said Mrs Dobson' I've been fucked for nothin' To cover himself he gave her an IOU. 'When will this become due' said Mrs Robson Dobson. 'Christmas' said ~~Churd~~ Churchill. 'Christmas?' said Mrs Dobsan' That ten bloody months owin' 'So it is' said Churchill' (can't wait that long' said Mrs Dobson. 'Well, I <u>can</u>' said Churchill and buggerd off. He went to ten Downing Street as he lives there rent free. Churchill was short of money all of his life. and even after that

Note: words missed out and words not completed – Spike would give this version to me to 'do whatever you have to do with it'. Most often with a note: 'Please ignore spelling – I did.'

'Darling, you must stop buying black silk underwear'
said Clemtine. 'why' said Churchill, 'no one can see
them'! They're too expensive dear'! 'Lissh' said
Churchill 'I'm Prime Minister of England, if I can't
afford it, who can?, eh?, eh?. 'But at the end of the
month we're broke' said Clemtine. 'I've been in tighter
spots than that' he laughed. 'We'll were over drawn at
the bank by ten thousand pounds. 'Well I've been in
tighter spots than _that_' he said lighting a Havana Cigar
and sipping a brandy. 'Lord Beaverbrook is going
to give me ten thousand pounds for writing
an article on life in the Artic' he said.
'You've never been to the Artic' said Clemtine
'Ah but he doesn't know that.' said Churchill
'Thats cheating' said Clemtine stamping her
foot, and breaking her anckle' 'Now look
what you've made me do' she said
limping away. 'I didn't _make_ you do it
growled Churchill' 'You'd betta lie down'
he suggested. 'Wot good that do's she
said. 'It will get you out of the bloody
way' he said pushing her back . Juss then
came the drone of a German plane.
'Quick phone the R.A.F and tell them
to shoot it down . A bomb landed
next to Churchill and blew him
backward out of his boots
thru a window, he landed
on a dustman in the act
of emptying a bin 'Coor Blimey
Winston Churchill' he gasped
'Wat a way to meet you'.
'the smell of the dustmen
awoke Churchill away
'Bloody snob' shouted the
dustman after him. Churchill
shouted something back but
was to far away to be
heard it was in fact
the words 'Bollocks'

'I did'nt <u>make</u> you do it growled Churchill. 'You'd better lie down' he suggested.

Wat good that do? she said

'It will get you out of the bloody way' he said pushing her back. Just then came the drone of German plane. 'Quick, phone the RAF and tell them to shoot it down.

A bomb landed next to Churchill and blew him backward out of his boots thru a window, he landed on a dustman in the act of emptying a bin 'Cor Blimey Winston Churchill' he gasped 'Wat a way to meet you'

'The smell of the dustman drove Churchill away

'Bloody snob' shouted the dustman after him.

Churchill shouted something back but was to far away to be heard it was in fact the word 'Bollocks'

Of course, thousands of miles away, Gandhi was resting and fasting and dying after his salt march to the sea he was laying on a rush mat in a room at the Indian YMCA.

'You must eat or you will die' said his European follower Mrs Gladys Squirt

'Thank you for the warning' said Gandhi collapsing to the floor

'Here eat this mango' she said

'They give you boils' said Gandhi

'Not right away' she said ramming one down his throat,

choking, he coughed up the stone'.

'Im sorry I forgot to take out' she said to the unconscious figure on the floor, with hot baths, massage, electric shock treatment and a five course meal Gandhi recovered enough to sit up and play play with himself. I must save India 'he said first we must kill all the whites.'

'I thought you were non violent' she said, kissing his feet

'While your down there can you cut my toe nails'

'I have'nt any scissors' she said

'Then bite them off'

'Im not biting any wogs toe nails' she retorted, tossing her head and catching as it came down

'Whats life about' said Nehru.

'Its about 70 for women and 65 for men' she said.

Of course, thousands of miles away, Ghandi was resting and fasting and dying after his salt march to the sea, he was laying on a rock mat in a room at the Indian YMCA. "You must eat or you will die" said his European follower Mrs Gladys Squirt, "Thank you for the warning" said Ghandi collapsing to the floor. 'Here eat this mango' she said 'They give you Goils' said Ghandi " ; ; Not white, right away" she said ramming one down his throat & choking he coughed up the stone. ' I'm sorry I forgot to take it out' she said to the unconscious figure on the floor, with hot baths, massage, electric shock treatment and a five course meal Gandhi recovered enough to sit up and play play with himself.. I must save India' he said first we must kill all the whites. ' I thought you were non violent," she said kissing his feet 'While your down there can you cut my toe nails." ' I have no scissors' she said 'then bite them off " ' I'm not biting any warts and catching as it came down' toe nails' she retorted, tossing her head 'whats life about' said Nehru, " $ts.70 for women and 65 for men' she said. Nehru realised he was $5 so immediately dropped down dead 'One down ten to go' said Mahatma placing Nehru on a pyre setting fire to it and floated it down the Ganges he floated out to sea where he was hit by 88 nary and sank next time, the heat from the fire revived him, and he vowed the burning pyre back to the shore, where he was treated for burns and malaria and starvation, he wored n't eat anything said he was slimming loosing 20 pounds a day on the 7th day he disappeared But reappear a month late in a num cell in the covent of Jesus + Mary, Poona

Nehru realised he was 65 immediately dropped down dead.

'One down ten to go said Mhatma, placing Nehru on a pyre setting fire to it and floated it down the Ganges he floated out to sea where he was hit by SS Mary and sank not him, the boat. The heat from the fire revived him, and he rowed the burning pyre back to the shore, where he was treated for burns and malaria and starvation, he would'nt eat anything said he was slimming loosing 20 pounds a day on the seventh day he dissappeared But reappear a month later in a nun cell in the convent of Jesus Mary, Poona

The nun was in bed and took the opportunity of dragging him in and screwing 'That's better,' she said 'Better' he said theres never been anything wrong with it'. Well he had now because she'd given him a dose. Shes a bloody Catholic! Three injections of Penicillin cleared the dose. But he swore never to co-habit with a nun again. Out of boredom he stowed away on a tramp steamer crewed by a mixture of far eastern cut-throat, They did'nt cut his throat but screwed the ass off him, in desperation he dived overboard and swam ashore and landed on a cannibal island where he was boiled and eaten with chips. His son Don came searching for him, he was very skinny, so was captured by the cannibals and put on a full fat diet, in preparation for boiling and eaten, alas he worried so much he never fattened, so they let him go, but where to go, he chose his native land Ireland he was welcomed home by a crowd of Irish idiots, recently released from the asylum due to over crowding.

'Come wid me Ive someting to show you' He showed him teapot, it was someting but that was all

'Its not very interesting' he said hitting the Irish idiot he didn't know that the idiot was a Karate expert, and ended up hurled into a tree, 'Get me down,' he shouted so the idiot sawed thru the branch Don was sitting on till it collapsed, crashing Don to the ground – and a hospital Alas the hospital was Pychaitric full of loonies, and tried to sell his bed to him for a million pounds

THE END

The nun was in bed and took the opportunit. of drugging him on and screwing" "Thats better," she said' Better' he said "theres neva been anything wrong with it'. Well he had now knew she'd given him a dose. She a bloody Catholic! Three injections of Penacillin "cleared the dose. But he swore neva to co-habit with a nun again. Out of boredum he stowed away on a tramp steamer crewed by a mixture of far eastern cut-throats, they didint cut his throat but screwed the cure off him, in desperation he dived overboard and swam ashore and landed on a cannibal island where he was boiled and eaten with chips. His son Don came searching for him, he was very skinny. so was captured by the cannibals and put on a full fat diet, in preparation for boiling and eaten, alas he worned so much he never fattened, so they let him go, but where to go, he chose his native land Ireland he was welcomed home by a crowd of Irish idiots, recently released from the asylum due to over crowding. ' Come wid me 'I've cemetary to show you' He showed him teapot, it was something but that was all " Its not very interesting' he said hitting the Irish idiot, he didint know that the idiot was a Karate expert, and ended up hurled into a tree, 'Get me down' he shouted & so the idiot sawed thru the branch Don was sitting on till it collapsed, crashing Don to the ground- and hospital Atn the hospital was psychiatric full of loonies, one tried to sell his had to him for a milleon pounds

57

His office: I called it his womb. It was chaos but he knew exactly where everything was.

1956: Chatham Empire. Peter, Spike and Max Geldray.

Spike and Eric in their office (collar and ties), 1954. They shared an office for 50 years.

STORIES FOR CHILDREN

THE GREAT BIM-BOM Childrens Circus.

Every ~~body~~ body at the Bim-bom Childrens Circus
was very excited they were going to perform
at London Towns ~~Hampst~~ famous Hampstead
Heath - the seats were full of children
who were full of jelly babies - suddenly
the Bim-Bom band struck up under its ~~leader~~
conductor Fred Nose, Omm pah-pah went
the Tuba played by Dick Twit, Tootely Toot
went Doris Cabbage, on the flute, she blew
so hard the elastic in her knickers broke and
they fell down - then Ben Barmy the drummer
hit his bass drum Boom-~~Crash~~ Boom - Crash
oh dear, he split the drum skin and inside
$\rightarrow 100$
he found a tiny door mouse, he ran up Ben's
trousers and bit him on the ~~bottom~~ bottom.
Now a big spot light shines on the
sawdust arena - and Tara-! on comes
the ring-master Captain Custard - ~~oh~~
~~how~~ he wears a red coat the same
colour as ~~his has nose~~ daddys nose, a
big black top hat, white trousers and blue
riding boots, all the children clap him
clap clap clapity clap, all except one little girl 173

THE GREAT BIM-BOM CIRCUS

Everybody at the Bim-Bom Childrens Circus was very
excited, they were going to perform at London Towns
famous Hampstead Heath – the seats were full of
children who were full of jelly babies, suddenly
the Bim-Bom Band struck up under it's conductor
Fred Nose, Omm pah-pah went the Tuba played by
Dick Twit, Tootley Toot went Doris Cabbage on the
Flute, she blew so hard the elastic in her knickers
broke and they fell down – then Ben Barmy the drummer
hit his bass drum, Boom Boom – Crash Oh dear! he
split the drum skin and inside he found a tiny door-
mouse, he ran up Ben's trousers and bit him on the
bottom.

Now a big spot light shines on the sawdust arena
and Ta-ra on comes the ring-master, Captain Custard
he wears a red coat the same colour as daddys nose,
a big black top hat, white trousers and blue riding
boots, all the children clap him, clap clap clapity
clap, all except one little girl called Rosemary
she clapped when she had an ice cream in one hand
and it all splashed out and went in a little boys
ear hole.

Captain Custard cracked his long whip and it caught
him on the back of his neck, he let out a yell and
his hat fell over his eyes – "Ladies and Children
Bim-Bom Circus proudly presents, Crimple the Crown-
the – Oh I'm sorry, I meant Pimple the Clown".

cal'd Rosemary she clapped when she had an
Ice cream in one hand ad and it all splashed
out and went in a little boys ear hole.
Captain Custard cracked his long whip, and
it caught him on the back of his neck he
let out a yell. and his hat fell over his eyes –
"Ladies + Children Bim-Bom Circus
proudly presents Pimple the Crimple the
Crown-the-oh Im sorry I meant Pimple
the Clown – Taa-raa – went the band and
Pimle came on – he did 20 Summer saults
and 10. Winter ones – he did a hand stand
'100 ➔
a fool stand and an impression of a hat stand
in a funny voice he said How do you do-
do do you how – then like magic he took
10. Big Sun flowers out of his trousers
and he balanced them on his head, his
nose, his knee – then he walked off on his
hands – Then Ta rara – Captain Custard
cracked his whip and caught him self on
the bumm! Ow! he went, and his eyes watered –
"Now" he said "we have the mighty Pakistan
Curry muscles"! Oh! on came a very strong
man – very very strong – he even smelt strong 203

Taa-raa - went the band and Pimple came on, he did
twenty summer saults and ten winter ones, he did
a hand stand, a foot stand an an impression of a
hat stand. In a funny voice he said, "How do you
do - do do you how" - then like magic he took ten
big sun flowers out of his trousers and he balanced
them on his head, his nose, his knee then he walked
off on his hands - Then, tar-ara - Captain Custard
cracked his whip and caught himself on the bumm!
Ow! he went and his eyes watered.

'Now' he said "We have the mighty Pakistani Currymuscles"
Oh! on came a very strong man - very very strong -
he even smelt strong. He showed his huge muscles
and the children clapped, and a little boy got more
ice cream in his ear hole. Mr. Currymuscles said
"Ladies and Children I now break world Guinness Book
record, I swallow 100 pounds of Mars bars", and in
one gulp they were gone - you could hear them going
down into his belly - rustle, rustle they went
because he forgot to take the wrappers off! "Ladies
and Children" he announced "I feel sick". Then he
bent down and grabbed two big purple dumb bells,
(they could'nt speak) "I now lift up 10 million tons"
with a big strain, his knees knocking, his eyes
crossed, he lifted the 10 million tons up and split
his trousers 'Ha ha ha' laughed the children.

He showed his huge muscles and the children clapped, and a little boy got more ice cream in his earhole, mr Curry muscle said "Ladies and Children -. I now break world Guiness Book record, I swallow 100 pounds of Mars bars, and in one gulp they were gone - you could hear them going down into his belly - rustle-rustle they went because he forgot to take the wrappers of. "Ladies and Children" he announced "I feel sick" - then he bent down and grabbed 2 big purple weights dumb bells (they couldn't speak" I now lift up 10 million tons", with big strain he knees knocking, his eyes crossed, he lifted the weight 10 million tons up and split his trousers, "Ha Ha Ha" laughed the children - then a spot light went on the top of the tent and it showed a tight rope - and waiting to go on was a clown in a red suit with white bobbles on - "A big hand for Willy Wibble Wobble Wobble" So some one gave Captain Custard a big hand Willy Wobble Wibble Wobble

171

Then a spot light went on the top of the tent and
showed a tight rope, and waiting to go on was a
clown in a red suit with white bobbles on. "A big
hand for Willy Wibble-Wobble," so someone gave
Willy Wibble Wobble a big hand, but he already
had two, so he put it in his pocket, then got on
his blue wheel and whizzed across the wire and back
the children clapped, more ice cream in the little
boys ear.

Now while the circus was going on - outside in a
tent was a real gypsy called Vera Fatlegs, who
could tell your fortune - a little boy called
Tom Lumps went in, the gypsy told him his fortune,
it came to 30p, well she charged him 30p so Tom Lumps
went away with no fortune at all.

but a big hand, but he already had two so he put it
in his pocket, then he got on his blue wheel wheel
and whizzed across the wire and back — the
children clapped, more ice cream in the little bag ear
Now while the circus was going on — outside
in a tent was a real gypsy lady called Vera Fatlegs who could
tell your fortune — a little boy call. Tom lumps
went in. the gypsy told him his fortune. it came
to 30P, well she charged him 30P so. he went
Tom lumps went away with no fortune at all. 100

Back in the Bim Bom Circus Captain Custard
had caught his neck a crack again as he
announced 'ladiessiss & Childrennnm — a very
dangerous act — all the way from Wistambul
we have Smelly Sam from Turkey — the band
played some Turkish delight music and came
Smelly Sam with his head a bandaged up
on the NHS, he had a long mustache that
finished behind his head, he had five long
sticks of liquorice with fire on the end
he poked the fire in his mouth and
screamed then he swallowed. the fire
ate the liquorice ate the liquorice and went 198
home. for a drink of water

Back in the Bim-Bom Circus Captain Custard had caught
his neck a crack again as he announced 'Ladiessiss and
Childrennnn a very dangerous act - all the way from
Wistambul - we have Smelly Sam from Turkey' - the band
played some Turkish delight music and on came Smelly
Sam with his head bandaged up on the NHS, he had a
long moustache that finished behind his head, he had
five long sticks of liquorice with fire on the end,
he poked the fire in his mouth and screamed, then he
swallowed the fire, ate the liquorice and went for
a drink of water. The children all clapped alot
clap + 10,000 they went. Now all the lights went
out and a big spot light showed a little Elephant
called Trinkle Trunk - and on his back was a clown
in blue, his hame was Tinkle Tonk, the elephant
raised his trunk and went 'Whoo whee woo' and ran
round and round the ring while Tinkle Tonk juggled
with coloured oranges, as Trinkle Trunk ran around,
the children laughed as his bottom wobbled like a
jelly, then Trinkle Trunk stood on his back legs,
Tinkle Tonk went on juggling but fell off "You naughty
naughty naughty naughty elephant". But the elephant
just dipped his trunk in a bucket of water and squirted
it all over him - then there was a little interval and
girls went around selling ice cream to the children,
all except one little boy who had enough in his ear.

the children all clapped a lot. clap+ 19 000
they went, now all the lights went out
and a big spot light showed a little
Elephant call Trinkle-Trunk- and on his back
was a clown in blue his name was Tinkle. tonk
the elephant raised his trunk and went "Whee whoo
Whee Woo" and ran round and round the ring
while Tinkle-tonk juggled with coloured oranges
as the Trinkle Trunk ran around the children
laughed as his bottom wobbled like a Jelly
then Trinkle Trunk stood on his back
legs, Tinkle Tonk went on juggling but fell off
"You naughty naughty naughty naughty
elephant" But the elephant just dipped his
trunk in a bucket of water - and squirted
it all over him - then there was a
little interval and girls went around
selling ice creams to the children all except
one little boy who had enough in his ear.
Then Tara bang crash roar - "ladies +
Children the last act is Golden Growl
the lion and his trainer Tinkle Tonk again -
there was a great roar a Golden Growl
leaped into the ring and showed his teeth

Then, Ta-ra bang crash roar - 'Ladies and Children
the last act is Golden Growl the lion and his
trainer, Tinkle Tonk again', there was a great
roar as Golden Growl leaped into the ring and
showed his teeth, Tinkle Tonk showed his teeth but
on one clapped. Tinkle Tonk made Golden Growl leap
in the air and twist his tail - then 'Oh dear!'
Tinkle Tonk put his head in Golden Growl's mouth
then he could'nt get it out - then Golden Growl
sneezed and Tinkle Tonks head fell, he made
Golden Growl promise never to do it again - then
he said "Give a savage growl for the children",
'GROWWELLLLLL' went Golden Growl but it made him
feel giddy and he had to sit down.

Then there was a great roll on the drum, and the
drummer ate it.
'Ladies and Children', said Captain Custard, 'for the
grand finale here are all the turns' - and on came
Pimple the Clown, Currymuscles, Willy Wibble Wobble,
Smelly Sam, Vera Fatlegs, Trinkle Trunk, Golden Growl,
and Tinkle Tonk, they all stood on each others shoulders
and sang God Save the Queen, and the children all went
home happy.

Tinkle Tonk showed his teeth but no one clapped
Tinkle Tonk made Golden Growl leap in the
air and twist his tail - then oh dear -
Tinkle Tonk put his head in Golden Growls
mouth then he couedint get it out -
the Golden Growl sneezed an Tinkle Tonks
head fell, he made Golden Growl promise
never to do it again — then he said "Give
a savage growl for the children
GROWWLLULL went Golden Growl
but it made him feel giddy and he had
to sit down - Then there was a great foo
roll on the drum· and the drummer ate it.
"Ladies and Children said soft Captain
Custard - for the grand finale here are
all the tums - and on came Pimple the
Clown, Currymuscles, Willy Wibble Wobble
Smelly Sam, Vera Fat legs, Trinkle Trunk
Golden Growl + Tinkle Tonk, they all stood on
each others shoueders and sang God Save
the Queen, and the Children all went home
happy.
              The End

December 1954: Camden Theatre. A *Goon Show* rehearsal. Back row: Wallace Greenslade, Harry Secombe. Front row: Peter Eton (producer), Spike, good-looking Eric Sykes..

Nod the Snail

Once upon a time there was a mummy snail and a daddy snail, they lived in
some rocks in the corner of the garden, and they came out at night to
eat some vegatable leaves, they weret very ordinary snails and like all
snails moved very very slowly, but then they had a baby snail, and he was
called Nod, he was a very ordinary snail and grew up to be just as slow
as his mother and father, until one day, there were some men working in
the garden, they were mending an electric wire, and one night Snod was
crawling over the wire when suddenly "FLASHHHHHH.. WHOOSHHHHHH? he touched the
live electric part and Nod shone like an electric light bulb, and suddenly
he started to move about so fast, he zoomed around the garden like a
motor scooter, when the people from the house went into their garden next morn
-ing, they saw them this snail go whosssshhhhh, past them ,then whossh back
again, then whoosh up to the top of the tree and the whooosh down again,
he was going so fast no one could see what it was, so they got a net trap and
put it in the garden , sure enough suddenly whoosh Snod came rushing by
and whooshe, he went right thru the net net, so next they dug a hole in the
garden and put along came Nod, and whoosh, he went right over
the whole to the other side and dissappeared across a field, so they
called the Police, the family said "Look theres something very small and
fast that rushes thru our garden, it frightens all the cats and dogs and
chickens and all the old grannies whose knickers fell down! Nod went so fast he whizzed up the
Motorway at a hundred miles an hour, he past everything, some people
who were driving their cars suddenly all shouted, "Help, look, theres
a snail going past us at a hundred miles an hour, so they told the police
and the =police gave chase in very fast motor-cars and with a special box they
caught Nod, imagine their suprise when they saw that Nod was a snail,
"The policeman said " Oh dear, its only a little snail, how can he go so fast!
" Soon Nod was very famous, because he was the fastest snail in the world,
so he got his picture in the newspapers, and he even went on television,
and he was on (NAME OF CURRENT CHILDRENS TV SHOWS), Now over in America
they have world champion snail races, and the winnder gets a Gold cup and 50p, so they entered him
for the race, and they took him by Concorde Jet plane, in a little box.
In the race were ten other champion snails, and came the great day , they
were all lined up ready for the race, the starter said" Ready- steady go",. and

off went the snails, but then whoshhhhhhh,and ~~Nodx~~ Nod shot over the finish

line,no one could believe it, all the other snails were still right at the

~~other ends~~, so Nod ~~xxxdx~~ won 50p and a Gold cup,/the Police took him   *start !*   and he went to meet President Regan the Boss of America, then

back to England and he went on Television with Terry Wogan,and he was

on the News, but really Nod wanted to be back in his garden with his mum and

dad, so he stopped going fast, and moved very slow like other snails,

every body was very worried about him, they took him to a snail doctor

who said "Theres nothing wrong with Nod, all snails move slow like him"

But they said "He <u>used</u> to go very <u>fast</u>" and the snail doctor said "Well thats

when he must have been sick, because snails <u>don't</u> go fast, so now hes

going slow, *means* hes better". So the police took him back to his garden and let hi

—m go, and there he met his mum and dad again, and they were so happy to see

him, because they thought he was dead, and they took him home and they had

a lovely snails dinner of lettuce leaf and *chips.* ~~lettuce leaf and sugar~~

The story is written to include, counting,textures,descriptions,moral justice,
sentoment,family togetherness. Nota Bene: Certain words are underlined, and in
reading they should be stressed to give emotional bite to the story.

T H E - S Q U I R R E L - F A M I L Y .

Once upon a time there lived a lovely Red squirrel called Charles,he

had a beautiful warm red furry coat,and a big bushy tail big and red

like teachers nose, Charles was married to a lovely lady squirrel

called Lady Di,they lived in a Oak Tree, and this tree was nearly

three hundred years old, it was so big, it would take twenty children

holding hands to go round it. Charles and Lady Di had found a lovely
                         to make their home in,
big hole high up the top of the tree/ and sometimes Charles would sing

a song and he and Lady Di would do break dancing, sometimes they would

break a chair sometimes a table .Charles loved Lady Di very much and

one day Lady Di told Charles she was going to have a baby and he fain

-ted and went BONK! on the ground, so Lady Di poured a bucket of cold

water over him and he felt much better. Together they made a little bed

of nice clean dry grass and they put daisy flowers all the way around

for when the baby squirrel was born and Lady Di started to knit a pair

of silly-socks for the baby ,because any squirrel wearing socks would

look silly. Charles went off to collect plenty of nice fresh nuts so

there would be plenty of food for when the baby arrived, Charles liked

collecting nuts, most of his friends were nuts. One morning the baby
                                                              t
was born, and when Lady Di told Charles he fainted again and BONK on

the floor,but after she threw a bucket of water over him he was much

better. The baby squirrel was a boy, and they called him Little Willy.

Little Willy was sooo little, just the size of your thumb. Lady Di ga
                                 r/
-ve him lots of milk to drink, and Charles said I think you're giving
                                     "
him too much cows milk and Lady Di said"Why" and Charles said because
                             "|
he keeps going Moooo-Mooooooo! Soon the Summer came and Charles and I
                               to teach him how to
-ad Di took little Willy for walk along the tree branch, and Charles
                                   on
fell off and went Bonk on the ground,so Lady Di threw a bucket of water

over him and he felt much better. Soon little Willy was big enough to

walk on the branches alone, but Lady Di had told him "Be very careful,

100

that some big bird or a pussy cat does'nt catch you and eat you up",
—Bird
and, there was a big black crow called Rotten·Dicky/who tried to catch

little Willy by the tail, but then brave daddy Charles came out and

shouted "If you touch my little Willy again, I'll set fire to your
tail feathers and burn your bottom"!
tree and you'll have boiled eggs in your nest", "Caw" said the crow

because that was the only word he knew. Then one day Little Willy fell

out of the tree and broke his leg, but an old gardner, Tom Sillybom, saw

poor little Willy and said "Oh dear" he picked poor little Willy up

but OUCHHHHHHHH Willy bit him on the finger, so, Tom had to put on

anti-squirrel gloves and took Willy to the vets Mrs Funnyconk, she

put little Willys leg in plaster and put him in a box near the fire,

poor little Willy was so sad. His poor mum and dad were looking every

where for him shouting "Little Willy, where are you", LadyDi was crying
                                                                  lost
and crying and crying and made the floor

all slippery and Charles slipped on it and went Bong on the ground. Tom
        the gardner
Sillybom, and his wife looked after Little Willy very well, but and son
Little Willys
soon/his leg was better, and he started to leap all over the house, o

-ne night, Mrs Sillybom got such a fright, because Little Willy had

jumped into a bowl of Jelly and Custard, Mrs Sillymom shouted "Helllp!

theres a jelly and custard with legs running round the room! One Sunday
                                         into
morning, they let Little Willy out in the garden and he ran straight

across the lawn and up the Old Oak tree to his mum and dad, and there

was Lady Di pouring a bucket of water over Charles and when they saw
                     With
him Charles fainted and he helped Lady Di pour a bucket of water over

him to make him feel better, and they all lived happily ever after until

Childrens Television Time.

Ⓢ

ARE YOU GOING TO GET AWAY WITH THIS

Ⓣ.

He laughed at my note and said, 'I always live in hope.'

A LIFE AFTER DEATH STORY FOR CHILDREN

Once upon a time there were two butterflies, with green, gold and red wings, they were called Mr. and Mrs. Lovely. One day Mrs. Lovely laid two little white butterfly eggs under a leaf, so the rain wouldn't give them a cold, after a few days the eggs hatched and out came two brown and yellow spotted hairy caterpillars, they looked round; one was called Ding, and the other was called Dong, when they stood together they were Ding-Dong. Ding said: "I'm so happy being a caterpillar".

"So am I" said Dong.

"We are both young, and we are going to have a lovely time eating nice green leaves, playing caterpillar games, and lying in the sun and sleeping in the moon". They had a super time, sometimes birds tried to eat them, but no! Ding and Dong looked all smellypoo - and the birds didn't want to. Ding and Dong used to eat a hundred leaves a day! They were very happy, but one day, they both started to feel very strange, they got all sleepy and they didn't feel happy anymore, their friend, a big black beetle called Tiggle Toggle said, "I think you are both going to die!".

"Oh dear" said Ding, "Oh Ding", said Dong. "What happens when we die" said Ding.

"Well" said the black beetle called Tiggle Toggle, "Some people say you go to heaven".

"What's heaven like?" said Ding and Dong.

"I don't know" said Tiggle Toggle. "people say it's a place where God lives and when you die you go there and he makes you happy".

"We don't want to die" said Ding and Dong. "We're <u>already</u>
happy". Then a deep voice said "There's no such place as
heaven".

They looked up and there was a big black vulture called
Lumpy-conk.   "When you die that's the end of you", he
said and flapped his wings.

Poor Ding and Dong cried - the next week Ding and Dong fell
asleep, and slowly they turned into dirty brown cocoons.

They stopped moving and became very still.   "Yes, they're
dead said Lumpy-Conk.   "I8m going to eat them all up".

But Tiggle Toggle the beetle said "Don't you dare!"if you
do I'll bang you on the beak with a conk-hammer.

This frightened off Lumpy-Conk who flew away to his nest to
play his banjo.

All winter the two little cocoons of Ding and Dong lay
still, stuck to the leaves and everybody said "Poor things,
they haven't moved for over a year, they must be dead".

and everybody forgot all about them except Tiggle Toggle
the beetle, who came once a month and put little forget-
me-not flowers by the bodies.   But, one sunny day, Tiggle
Toggle was walking along a branch to put flowers on Ding
and Dong when he saw something <u>magic</u> happening!

The two little coffins of Ding and Dong split open ....
and out came two beautiful butterflies, scarlet and green
and purple.

3

"Whoopee" said Ding and Dong.   "Look at us! We're not
dead anymore" and they flew up and down the garden drinking
honey from the flowers and playing aeroplanes.

"Tiggle Toggle was right" said Ding.   "This is better than
being a hairy caterpillar".

Tiggle Toggle the beetle was right, there is a heaven, and
they flew through the summer gardens with thousands and
thousands of coloured flowers.

The Cat.

My wife to be ~~the~~ ~~Be~~ Tessa Jones and I were standing at the altar about to be married – the vicar was about to say I now pronounce man and wife when the Cat. A Black cat appeared at the altar! My instinct was to bend down and stroke it. But no, the moment I touched it, it snarled, and lashed at me with her claws, it drew a long red bloody scratch on my hand while started to bleed. It's tore that and healed at me, until the priest drove it away. She said holding a crucifixe. She is the devil, a cat is at the devil! It's a cat, my Cat was trembling with fear. Balls! a scratches turned septic, they became serious, I was hospitalised, with a high temperate – penacellin I was given penacellin, penecellin, me a guitar players. All on 2d hours, It pelld my arm was amputated. The bloody thing that bloody cat – It disappeared, The bloody thing leaving me with one arm – I carried a small automatic pistol – if ever I saw that bloody cat!!!

28 Sept 99

20·14 20

Sam

I'm here God.

Where are you

One night coming out of a Pub, I·e· saw the cat, east by a cars head lights. My God was I imaging it, he was a big as a large dog, in fact the size of a panther, I drew my pistol, but he was gone. In the following weeks – news paper spoke of the killing of sheep by a large animal, believed to be a panther that had escaped from the zoo, pot armed police patrols were looking for it. A month later, December, it was freezing. ~~There was a tap at~~ I was seated before a blazing log fire. Something drew my attention, my God it was the huge cat, it scratched at the window, it wanted to come in. I reached for my revolver, and upead the window, it came in very smoothly, cat like, and the lay in front of the fire, I sat there fascinated there was a knock on the door, it was a policeman " we have followed the beast sir to here " Yes I said than awkardly. "Yes its asleep by the fire" Can I come in sir" he said cocking hispistol. Taking aim he shot

PTO

105

The beast it gave a premium howl.
the became smaller and smaller - and
disappeared. leaving only a bird stand
Carpet

Sent To S.M.

THE CAT by Spike Milligan   27-10-99

My wife to be Tessa Jones and I were standing at the altar about
to be married - the vicar was about to say I now pronounce ~~man~~ You
and wife when the Cat a black cat appeared at the altar. ~~My~~
My instinct was to bend down and stoke it but no, the moment I
touched it it snarled backed away and lashed at me with his claws,
it drew a long red bloody scratch on my hand which started to
bleed it stood there and hissed at me until the priest drove it
away holding a crucifix. "She is the devil" he said in a voice
trembling with fear. Balls the cat isn't the devil it's a cat my
scratch has turned septic they become serious. I was hospitalised
with a high temperature I was given penicillin,penicillin,penicillin
it felt my arm was complete me a guitar player. All in 24 hours
that bloody cat it disappeared the bloody thing leaving me with one
arm. I carried a small automatic pistol if ever I saw that bloody
Cat!!!
One night coming out of a pub I saw the Cat cast by a cars headlights.
My God was I imaginging it he was as big as a large dog,in fact the
size of a panther I drew my pistol but he was gone. In the following
weeks newspapers spoke of the killing of sheep by a large animal
believed to be a panther that had escaped from the zoo armed police
patrols were looking for it. A month later,December,it was freezing
I was seated before a blazing log fire something drew my attention
my God it was the huge cat it scratched at the window it wanted to
come in. I reached for my revolver and opened the window it came
in very smartly, cat like, and the lay in front of the fire I sat
there fascinated there was a knock on the door it was a policeman
"We have followed the beast Sir to here" "Yes" I said then awkwardly
"Yes it's over by the fire" "Can I come in Sir" he said cocking
his pistol taking aim he shot the beast it gave a piercing howl then

became smaller and smaller and disappeared leaving only a blood
stained carpet.

DOLORES. TYPED THIS: ITS O.K.

VERY BAD
JELLY

BAD JELLY WAS MENDING her broom stick watched by Devil, the evil black cat, who was playing with a dead mouse.

Oh, why don't you eat' said Bad Jelly.

'Im not hungry' moaned Devil.

Then give it to Horrid the Hairy dog.'

'Hes out hunting rabbits' said Devil. 'Hes trying to catch one for you to cook for dinner to night.

But Devil was old and could'nt catch a Rabbit so she went to the fishmongers a bought a fish.

Bad Jelly II ate the fish bones and all Help!

Ive got a fish bone in my throat' so they lowered willy the worm down with a hook to pull it out.

'Oh thank you willy it was very kind of you' and ate him up

Willy the worm in the witchs belly.

But Willy the worm found his way out the back. Where he was met by Grump the elf, who took to tea in a tree, but Gump gave Willy a magic mushroom and he turned into a crow But, the crow did'nt Caw but started meow.

Caw-meow-caw-meow, what next a crow cat?

Bad Jelly sat in her castle, watching a big cauldron coming to the boil 'Oh Im very hungry, I must go and get a boy or girl to eat

Jim and Rose were walking back from school thru the woods. 'Be careful said a friendly tree, theres a witch about, Just then Jim Rose were thrown in a sack by the witch

Tee-hee – cackled the witch. I'll have them for my supper and I'll give some to Devil my cat.

But Grump heard them calling Help that sounds like somebody in trouble, so he walked towards the sound of Help. Then he saw the sack with someone struggling to get out, so he got his Swiss Army knife, cut the string and out rolled Jim and Rose and a Duck!

'How did he get in' said Grump

'He was in here when we got on' The witch was going to eat him with us and chips' said Rose.

How many times did I say, 'Please, Spike, write me a follow-up to Bad Jelly'? Total lack of interest – until this arrived.

'You must be hungry' said Grump

'Yes, we're starving, we have'nt eaten for 3 days' said Rose

'Then you must force yourselves' said Grump. He took Rose Jim and the duck to his strawroofed cottage on top of a mountain. Sit at the table' he said

Then cooked them fried eggs and bacon an a big pot of tea Jim and Rose gobbled up the meal in 3 minutes.

'My you must have been hungry' said Grump 'Now you can have a sleep in my bunk beds'

'I'll have the top bunk' said Jim

'No, you wont' said Rose 'I'll have it'

'Oh don't argue over it' said Grump, 'Well toss for it heads or tails?'

'Tails said Rose but it came down heads so Jim slept in the top bunk. But they could'nt sleep because an owl kept hooting all night. Jim clamped his beak together with a clothes peg.

The owl was so angry he flew down and bit Jim on the bum

'Ow! My bum' shouted Jim 'Hes bitten my bum, but I can't see where'.

Never mind said Rose I'll put a plaster on it said Rose

But oh dear, the plaster came off in the bath 'Don't worry said Rose 'I'll kiss it better, so Rose kissed Jims bum better.

'You are a very good girl, not many sisters would kiss their brothers bum.

Yes she was a very brave girl,' said her mother 'Im going to tell the Queen about it. So she told the Queen 'Oh what a brave boy, bring him to the Palace' So Jim was presented at court, and the Queen gave him the Victoria Cross for bravery

That afternoon Jim and Rose were climbing trees, when they came across a crows nest, it had three eggs which were about hatch, as they did out flew 3 witches on broomsticks flew out heading for the moon. On the moon was a witches convention they were all preparing terrible spells that they would put on children, they were all dancing and screaming round a huge bonfire on which they were burning models of boys and girls 'Im going to eat three girls' screams a witch and Im going to boil three boys for soup screamed another with. Then the all jumped on their broom sticks and flew to the earth each wicked witch looking for a boy or girl to eat. Jim and Rose were asleep in Grump's cottage, Jim was dreaming of apple pie and Custard, Rose was dreaming of making dolls clothes. They were in bed because they had measles, Measles was an illness that witches were terrorfied of catching, as they flew in the window of Grumps cottage, they saw the measles a screamed with terror, but too late they caught measles and the measles caught them. The all had to go to a witchs measle hospital, so they would'nt fly away and spread it their broomsticks were all locked up

The witches started crying tears of acid, that burnt their clothes, making holes in them, so you could see in. They were crying for the return of their broomsticks, without them they could'nt fly anywhere and find boys and girls to eat 'I have'nt seen an witches for a while' said Jim

'No they must be tired' said Rose.

Witches dont get tired' said Jim, they run on batteries, they must be charging them.'

Yes, the witches broomsticks <u>were</u> battery charged with three speed gear Low - middle - fast, SUPER FAST, some witches broomsticks could do a 100 miles per hour, but they had to hold tight and put their seat belt on. If they exceed the speed limit the ZONE police would pull them over and fine the £50 for speeding. 'This is a violation of privacy' one screamed; who only had £49 pounds.

Jim and Robin were scrumping apples from a tree in the farmers field. They were delicious, very big a red a full of juice. They took some home to Grumpy and he made them into cider, it was very strong, and after drinking some Jim & Rose fell fast asleep. While they were in the land of Nod It snowed, and the whole countryside was blanketed in white. Using a sledge made by Grunge, the pulled each other around the field They found a hill, and that was it, they spent the whole day sledging down it. At the end of the day Grunges served them up with piping hot potatoe and Pea soup. That night they went to sleep by a roaring log fire. The world seem'd wonderful

It was Christmas week and it was snowing. Grung had a big sleigh pulled by two Reindeer. They went into Tinsel Town Christmas Shopping. Jim & Rose bought Grunge a pair of fleece lined slippers. On Christmas Eve they made a little Nativity scene, with baby Jesus in a straw cot. They heard someone singing carols at the front door they were Tree Goblins and their families with a lantern, Grunge gave them ten shillings, and they were so pleased the sang an extra Carol

Jesus bless this house

with its cat and mouse

They bought a Christmas from a Fairy Christmas shop, they did it all up with silver stars, little colored candles and shiny colored ball, then they wrapped all the presents in coloured paper, with big white labels, and waited for the day.

Christmas Eve, they all put their night clothes on sat around the fire and told Ghost stories. Then the cuckoo clock cuckooed nine, time for bed. As the night was cold Grung gave each of them a hot water bottle

They were so excited the could'nt sleep So Grunge gave them each a glass of hot mulled, and that sent them to sleep. While they were Grunge filled their stocking with little toys apples and nuts. It was such a happy morning Santa Claus had done his duty.

But Jim big present, was a big fort and a box of soldiers to (*original word is illegible*). It Rose had a lovely fairy doll, with three changes of costum They were so happy they hugged each other. Rose spent the day shampooing her dolls blonde hair. Jim spent the day getting his soldiers to capture the fort. It was a very happy. Suddenly in the fire place there was a blinding light, there sparkling bright was the Fairy Queen. 'Hello children, are you happy with the toys Santa brought you'?

'Oh yes, said the children, would you like to stay for a glass of wine'? Yes she would. She drank <u>three</u> glasses of wine and started to giggle. 'I better go before I get to tipsy' she said and vanished leaving behind a lovely smell of scent. So, with that ended the Children's Happy Christmas.

THE END

Very Bad Jelly. two.

Bad Jelly was mending her broom stick watched the Devil, her the euie black cat, who was playing with a dead mouse. Oh why don't you eat' said Bad Jelly. ' I'm not hungry' meiowed Devil, Then give it to Horrid the hairy dog.' ' Hes out hunting rabbits' said Devil ' Hes trying to catch one for you to cook for the dinner to-night.

Horrid

Devil

But Devil was old and could'nt catch a Rabbit, So she went to the fishmongers a bought a fish

Bad Jelly 11 ate the fish bones and all Help'

' Ive got a fish bone in my throat" so they lowered willy the worm down with a hook to pull it out.' Oh thank you willy it was very kind of you' and ate him up & Willy the worm in the witches belly

I was often asked whether I thought Spike was a genius. No, I didn't. But he had a great creative talent – a gift – in that he was able to sit down and write a poem or story with no hesitation. All in one go, as above.

But Willy the worm found his way out the back. where
he was met by Grump the   elf, who took to tea
in a tree, but Grump gave   willy a magic mushroom
and he turned into a crow   But, the crow did·nt cawl
but started meuow.

willy→ ⌐┼┼┐ ←Grump

Willy the
worm

Grump

Horrid

Caw - meow - Caw - meow, what next a crow - cat?

Bad Jelly sat in her castle, watching a big cauldron comin to the boil 'Oh I'm very hungry, I must go and get a boy or girl to eat. Jim and Rose were walking back back from school thru the woods, 'Be careful said a friendly tree, there's a witch about, Just then Jim & Rose were thrown in a sack by the witch

Tee-hee- cackled the witch, I'll have them for my supper and I'll give some to Devil my cat.

Help Help

But Grump heard them calling Help, thats sounds like somebody in trouble, so he walked towards the sound of Help. Then he saw the sack with someone struggling to get out, so he got his Swiss Army knife, cut the string and out rolled Jim and Rose and a Duck! 'How did he get in' said Grump 'He was in here when we got in' The witch was going to eat him with us and chips' said Rose "You must be hungry 'said Grump 'Yes we're starving, we have'nt eaten for 3 days' said Rose 'Then you must force yourselves' said Grump. He took Rose Tim and the duck to his straw roofed cottage on top of a mountain. Sit at the table' he said Then cooked them fried eggs and bacon on a big pot of tea, Jim and Rose gobbled up the meal in 3 minutes. 'my you must have been hungry' said Grump 'No'

you can have a sleep in my bunk beds" I'll have the top bunk"' said Jim ' No you won't 'said Rose 'I'll have it' 'On don't argue over it said Grump 'Well toss for it, heads or tails?' -Tails said Rose 'but it come down heads so Jim slept in the top bunk. But they couldnt sleep because an owl kept Hooting all night. Jim clamped his beak together with a clothes peg.

116

The owl was so angry he flew down and bit Jim on the bum 'Owl my bum' shouted Jim 'he's bitten my bum' but I can't see where". Never mind said Rose I'll put a plaster on it's and Rose But oh dear, the plaster came off in the bath" Don't worry said Rose, 'I'll kiss it better, so Rose kissed Jim bum better. " You are a very good girl, not many sisters would kiss their brothers bum. Yes she was a very brave girl" said her mother" I'm going to tell the Queen about it. So she told the Queen "Oh what a brave boy, bring him to the Palace" So Jim was presented at court, and the Queen gave him the Victoria Cross for bravery

That afternoon Jim and Rose were climbing trees, when they came across a crows nest, it had three eggs which were about hatch, as they did out flew 3 witches on broomsticks flew out heading for the moon. On the moon was a witches convention they were all preparing terrible spells that they would put on children, they were all dancing and screaming round a huge bonfire on which they were burning models of boys and girls 'I'm going to eat three girls' scream a witch and I'm going to boil three boys for soup scream another witch. Then the all jumped on their broom sticks and flew to the earth each wicked witch lookm for a boy or girl to eat. Jim and Rose were asleep in Grumps cottage, Jim was dreaming of apple pie and custard, Rose was dreaming of making dolls clothes. They were in bed because they had measles, measles was on their that witches were terrified of scratching catching, as they flew in the window of Grumps cottages they saw the measles a screamed with terror, but too late they caught measles and the measles caught them. The all had to go to a witches measle hospital, so they wouldn't fly away and spread it their broom sticks were all locked up

The witches started crying tears of acid, that burnt their for there
clothes, making holes in them, so you could see in. They were
crying for the return of their broomsticks, without them
they couldn't fly anywhere and find boys and girls to eat
'I have'nt seen em witches for a while said Jim 'No they must
be tired' said Rose. Witches dont get tired 'said Jim,
they run on batteries, they must be charging them".
Yes, the witches broomsticks were battery charged
with the three speed gear low - middle - fast   1 vo
SUPER FAST, some witches broom sticks could
do a 100 miles per hour, but they had to hold
tight and put their seat belt on - If they
exceed the speed limit the ZONE
police would pull them over and fine
the £50 for speeding' This is a violation
of privacy" one screamed who only had

£49 pounds.

Jim and Robin were scrumping apples
from a tree in the farmers field. They
were delicious, very big a red a full of
juice. They took some home to Grumpy
and he made them into cider, it
was very very strong, and after drinking
some Jim + Rose fell fast asleep.
While they were in the land of Nod
It snowed, and the whole countrysed.
was blanketed in white. Using
a sledge made by Grunge, the
pulled each other around the field
They found a Gully and that was
it, they spent the whole day
sledging down it. At the end of
the day Grunges served them
up with pop ing hot potatoes
and pea soup. That night they
went to sleep by a roaring log
fire the world seem'd wonderful
.

It was Christmas week and it was snowing. Grunge had a
big sleigh pulled by two Reindeer. They went into Tinsel
Town Christmas Shopping. Jim & Rose bought Grunge a
pair of fleece lined slippers. On Christmas Eve they
made a little Nativity scene, with baby Jean
in a straw cot. They heard some one singing Carols
at the front door, they were Tree Goblins and their
families with a lantern, Grunge gave them
ten shillings, and they were so pleased the sang

an extra Carol
        Jesus bless this home
        with its cat and mouse

They bought a Christmas from a Fairy Christmas
shop, then did it all up with silver stars, little colored candles
and shiny colored ball, then they wrapped all the presents
in coloured paper, with big white labels, and waited for

the day.

Christmas Eve, they all put their night clothes on
sat around the fire and told Ghost stories. Then
it was then the cuckoo clock cuckooed nine time
time for bed. As the night was cold Grunge gave
each of them a hot water bottle

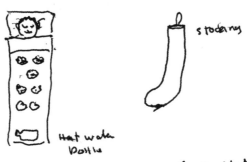

stocking

Hot water
Bottle

They were so excited the could'nt sleep
So Grunge gave them each a glass of hot
mulled, and that sent them to sleep.
While they were Grunge filled their
stocking with little toys apples and
nuts. It was such a happy morning
Santa Crouse had done his duty.

119

But Jim big present, was a big fort and a box of soldiers to mum. It Rose had a lovely fairy doll, with three changes of costom They were so happy they hugged each other. Rose spent the day shampooing her dolls blonde hair. Jim spent the day getting his soldiers to capture the fort. It was a very happy. Suddenly in the fire place there was a blinding light, there sparkling bright was the fairy Queen. "Hello children, are you happy with the toys Santa brought you? " "Oh yes, said the children, Would you like to stay for a glass of wine"? Yes she would. She drank three glasses of wine and started to giggle. " I better go before I get to tipsy" she said and vanished leaving behind a a lovely scent smell of scent. So, with that ended the the Childrens Happy Christmas.

The End

1960: The last series of the *Goon Show*. Spike reading his final script.

1967: A *Bed Sitting Room* rehearsal.

A MILLIGAN MISCELLANY

The BBC have asked me to write a hundred and fifty words to go along with this cassette. Fish, love cupboard ripe, leg, pencil, house, nail, teeth, kiss, flute, elephant giant, honey, rabbit, scouse, lamp, whistle, cup, clarionet horse, grain, Poona, rust, gutter, plimsole, hurt, dental client, musket, plinth, calf, mutton, if, no, but, fish nun, broom, ball, cliff, age, Kenneth, cob, slur, angle pin, dent, plinth, dog, ease, ear, lentil, nose, grey, desert, lino, glint, earth, dial, hair, dirt, porridge, note court, cannon, live, ant, garment, spook, cannon, diet, coke, oil, bustard, gannet, net, spice, lemon. guitar, string, dote, don't, minute, sterile, saint ranger, moon, coat, nether, lint, stamp, hand, oat, noon, kitten, earth, tea, party, lemon, lute, gong priest nonsense pickle brain, curve, rick, nest, dog easy fox. bolt, second, honk, doubt, curtain lid ache, axle, dolt, pun, liver, tin, milk, oboe, pink, ton wheel, buck, norman. dive, trap, trot, poke, big pound, lentil, soup, trundle, trap, ink, wad, tick, flute, note* telegraph, cart, bullock, pack, forage, cut, tin, lid, egg, seam, torrent, roger, vault, item, itch.

Spike. Milligan

* used twice for effect

I asked Spike to 'write 150 words' as an intro for a BBC cassette. This is what he sent me.

Quasi Modo. I can tell
That name that name
                The
with the holy at the rings a bell
                the bird.
Hes in the tower at Notre D.
                        Clifford
He rings the bell where ever he in
Hes such a ugly bugger
                with a
I' Hes got an empty back

<u>Quasi Modo</u>

Quasi Modo   I can tell
That name rings a bell
He rings the bell where ever
He rings the bell where
            t
Hes rings in the Notre Dame
He rings it where ever he am
Esmarald was the love of Quam
He was not good looking was he?

This is a perfect example of Box 18: scraps of paper and his reworking of Quasimodo.
They were published in *A Mad Medley of Milligan* – but I thought it was so typical.

The Leshic Laket Lee
Will be the death of me
& The Leshic Laket Lee
Is very hard to see
It attacks your head
Will your laying in bed
Does the leshic laket lee .
But I foiled the leshic laket Lee
By staying awake you see!

Lesic Loket Lee

The Lesic Loket Lee

Will be the death of me
The Lesic Lokit Lee
Is very hard to see
It attacks your head
when your laying in bed
I foiled the Lesic Lokit Lee
By staying awake you see!

Babu

Babu Babu
Indian Banker
People say hes just a wanker
He says, no I'm not
Look at the money I've got
So they looked at the money he got
And,
That was his lot.

Sea

I was walking by the sea
When it splashed me.
People with wet trousers
Are not welcome in peoples houses.
They might
The ~~even~~ laugh at me
But I'll blame it on the sea
See?

Being you - whats it like just being you
Just the thought of seeing you
Blows my mind away.
And your face
Like a fire in outer space
All the grace and the pace
Of the hundred meters
Hunting Cheethas
What to do
When you meet somebody who
Puts some kind of spell on you
Goes and rings the bell on you
Its hell on you
So then you just stand and wait
Like a beggar at the Palace gate
Hoping for that burning Satyr glance
A smile perchance.
The voice that sets your heart a-dance
I wish I knew
Just what its like.
Being you.

Written Feb 4..87

S Milligan
Mar. 88.

129

DATE:........30th August, 1990........TIME:........4-50 p.m.....

ATTENTION:........H.R.H. THE PRINCE OF WALES.................

COMPANY:..

FACSIMILE NO:..

FROM:........SPIKE MILLIGAN...................................

NUMBER OF PAGES (including front page):.....2..

IF YOU DO NOT RECEIVE ALL PAGES PLEASE ADVISE US IMMEDIATELY

9 ORME COURT,BAYSWATER,LONDON W2 4RL,ENGLAND.

Spike Milligan

Twas in the year of 1990 A.D.
That Prince Charles was struck down by a tragedy
Polo was his favourite game
And that is the fiend sport to blame
When taking a swing at the ball
He did to the ground fast fall
Landing there on his right arm
Which the fall did cause him to harm
He had broken a bone in two places
And could no longer put on his own braces
Worst he could not play the fiend Polo
Which made his spirits sink so low
And while living in one of their houses
Di had to help him on with his trousers
He was writing with his left hand
And not a word could anyone understand
So he booked into the N.H.S.
To try and ease his financial distress
And all the nation did pray
That his right elbow would be O.K.
And so we all hope with hand on heart
That his arm will not come apart
That the operation will be a success
And reported in the Daily Express

                                    WILLIAM McGONAGALL.

Spike and Peter Sellers loved William McGonagall. They used to send each other poems in his style. Spike sent this to Prince Charles when Charles broke his elbow playing polo.

Therewas a time when Bondi Beach was a swimmers and surfers
paradise - then came a day when a new pennant was raised,
it was called "The Shit Flag" it meant the current was
bringing sewage ashore - it took Europe 2000 years to
reach that level of pollution - it took Australia just
two hundred.
I first saw Australia in 1958, I'd say I caught it at a
stage just before the critical change that took place in
the ensuing 30 years which all but wiped out the old
Australia culminating in the winning of the America Cup
and the Bi-centenial - whether it was for better or worse
is a matter of opinion. In the immediate post-war years,
in the eyes of the western world, Australia was backwater,
it rarely appeared in or on the news save when there was
an England-Australia Test Match - will you bear in mind,
at the time, Australia, a country the size of the U.S.A.
had a population of 5,000,000, by no means was it a
commercial giant, but no one was starving, the people
still talked of England of 'Home' or 'Old Dart', the
feeling that Queen Victoria was not quite dead still
pervaded the older generations, thinking in modern
terms, bearing in mind Chinas unsolved dilemma of 1,000
million people - I'd say Australias 5,000,000 was just
about right - with the population stabalising at that
figure, the country's as yet unexploited mineral wealth
would be held in trust for future generations of Australia.
At that time my mother, an ordinary working class person
bore out my opinions when she wrote in 1953 "This wonderful
land of sunshine and plenty" - don't forget, the word
'plenty'. There were of course those who thought selling
Australian resources was good business. This was all right
with renewable resources, wool, butter, lamb, but it was
the selling of expendable minerals - iron, coal, destruction
of rain forest for wood chip etc, that will cause a short
fall for future generations, maybe 2-300 years, but it would
come. I will use my home town - Woy Woy as a microcosm of
change during those 30 years. In 1950, Woy Woy dreamed on
the Brisbane Waters, there was space, there was quiet,
the journey by steam train from Sydney took (change at
Hornsby) 2½ hours, a journey through the magnificent Kurangi
Chase. Individual compartments with buttoned upholstery,
water jugs, foot warmers, at Hawkesbury a man patrolled the
platform selling "Hawkesbury Oysters, Shilling a Jar".
When you steamed into Woy Woy - there'd be a coal fire in
the waiting room, a meat pie and floater stall on the
platform. Ron Widow and his taxi would usually be waiting
(if not you'd have a beer at the Railway Tavern). You'd

squeeze in and Ron would drop you off one by one, yarning
all the way "Mrs. Tinkers 'avin an operation fer her veins".
At home in Orange Grove Road, the night would be welcomed
by possoms in the white gum behind the house - there were
green tree frogs and blue tongued lizards - on the waters
black swans. In the middle was S$_t$. Huberts Island - across
the ripe up Daleys point were the pecked carvings of the
extinct Dharug tribe - in that quiet I wrote my first best
seller. It's all gone no more black swans, increased
population, more motor boats, water skis, electric open
plan trains, sealed green glazed windows, from 6.00 a.m.
'till 9.30 a.m. the commuter lunatics roar past my mother's
home, the tree is empty of possoms - green frogs - the
last blue tongue killed by domestic dogs. St. Huberts
Island built over by Hookers - even my appeal to Lady
Hooker received no reply - but then the population was now
15,000,000 as some people say "we're only 15,000,000 - a
long time ago someone said that in China, and so the Woy
Woy I knew perished under population pressure, or as some
say progress. I remember in 1953 an estate agent pointing
at the green hills around Brisbane Waters and saying "One
day they'll all be covered in houses" - he was right -
now what?

          I see barbaric sodium city lamps
          pretending they can see.
          They make a new mad darkness.
          Beyond their orange pools
            the black endlessness of time beckons,
          What, in that unseen dark tomorrow
            is waiting.......
          That iron tomorrow, coming on
            unknown wheels
          Who is the driver,
          Will he see me in time?

                    Woy-Woy
                    NSW
                    Oct. 1971

September 1972. The poem at the end of this was later included in *Small Dreams of a Scorpion*.

Crush hot-
-lips that feel for some others, and smothers.
Khol black-
  eyes tradeing abduction, seduction.
Smoke from a Gitane, in mid light
Bells. ~~church~~ a church telling mid-night
Bells;
And the scent of that par-fume lingers
Ikons.
    black face virgins ~~adoring~~ adorning,
    (~~████████~~)

Jade- is the light from the rue gasolaire

Is there some one out there

knows about this affair

Who can handle a
                            are
    Scandalé in Bohemia.

                            Spike Milligan.
                            July 8   1990

    for Duncan Lamont

Norma Dear
My Car is down
the SIDE OF THE
SYNAGOGUE —
CAN YOU FEED
METER.

ALICE, BLOODY
AWFUL

Love
Me

Premiere night of *Alice in Wonderland*. He played the Griffin. Obviously he didn't think much of it.

Bronte Parsonage

It seem'd I went there in a dream. I was on
tour with a variety show. I chose a dark Sunday evening,
in winter, a cold rain was falling when I ~~approached~~
the door of the Bronte Parsonage, there on a polished brass
plate was the words The Reverend Patrick Bronte, There
were no tourist about, when I pulled the ~~bell~~ door bell,
~~there was a rattling of keys~~
I heard a tinkling in the hall, ~~then the great dark~~
~~Oak door, and open~~ a rattling of bolts, and there stood
the care taker, Good-evening sir, my name is Spike
milligan, the name he knew, I said I knew it was late
and a Sunday and raining, but I ~~choose~~ especially chose
such an evening to visit the Parsonage, I knew well
the story of the Brontes, would he allow me a visit
of the building, he smiled and said 'Of course Spike' come
in. I felt comforted at him using my first name. In the
parlour was the chaise longue on it had died Emily Bronte.
In Charlottes bedroom was her bed made up on it
ready for the night, a cold wind was shaking the shutters,
that very sound Charlotte must have heard, The most
remarkable room was one in which en children they had
drawn in pencil, the lower-wall was full of them —
it was haunting – child haunting,
Now Anne, fearing death was near, wrote a
poem poignantly expressed, it began

A dreadful darkness closes in
On my bewildered mind
Oh let me not suffer, and not sin
Be tortured yet resigned.

I ~~too saw the bed in which she died.~~
~~Then Bramwells room very simple in it he had died~~
~~from drink and drugs. The Reverend Bronte family were~~
~~passing away~~

In an attempt to revive her, the family sent to an Hotel in Scarborough, Charlotte accompanied her, alas Anne died in one of the hotels rooms. Her grave is in the town the the disease affected Charlotte, , before the illness took hold she married Mr Nicholls, alas not long after Charlotte died . I shall never forget my visit to the Bronte Parsonage

Norma, included this in Vol 1 of my life story

WHAT LIFE STORY.

spike milligan

9, Orme Court,
London, W.2.

19th December, 1969

John Hyman, Esq.,

~~Dear John,~~ My dear John,

Take two of these before retiring, and then one three times a day; morning, lunch and early evening. They may make you feel thirsty, and give you a dry mouth, so keep a glass of water by the bed. Two days on these can't hurt you; might give you a little breathing space.

I have been on them four years, and they manage to keep me going. They are not addictive.

Let me know how you feel in a couple of days time. (Christ, I sound like the family doctor!)

Love, Light and Peace,

Spike

Spike

The caring Spike, when my husband (now ex) was ill.

Early Poems –

Where are you now
My beautiful love
Where oh where are you now

Does another posess you
Do other eyes distress you
And do you in the _night_...
Think of me
Of me and that sunny day
When we were young
And dreams came true

Those dreams that have gone

Gone – leaving only the dust of

a once great flame –

This was originally written hastily in pencil
in 1951 – to Toni Pontani

Dec 1 1900 Frustration

My mind is over-flowing
but its nowhere to go

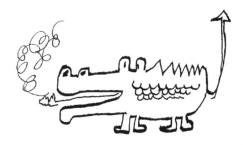

here with castle + dragon

(NO) 6/10 Could Do Boston
TALK TO ME

MENZIES

MELBOURNE

Norma dear child,
    Just read the attached!
Wow! Its no good. IIII have
to be beatified! make 4

2

thats all posh Gird.
send me back the original. I
want to gloat over it.!!!
                    Regards-
                As Ever-
                Spike

Spike happy with a write-up for once.

0442- 230627

One central point of fire and ice
A thousand moons melt down
There is a luminous
    diamond in my mind
The sharp edges tear the brain
Central a cobra sees to strike
please god can he do it soon

Ho park

Waiting - we are all waiting -
waiting for the waiting to stop

Please God,
    Please some one.
Let me light my candle.

Some where, somehow, A God
was trying to tie in a knot in
us, and we let him. A bird of
Paradise was flying, but with
different hues, we must have
been blind not to see him

Tabetha my furry dove
"   '   "   love
So How this family all were smitten
When you are here as a kitten
Now you have gone ~~afar~~ to Valhalla
Killed By a speeding motor·car
~~By a speed~~

I saw you
At Moondazzle
~~And you were there~~
Roll right stones
In the dark
In the rain
the bird of night
empty of song

Gondarland together again
there are no ~~frontiers~~
We together again
this awful penalty
for living, called
Death —
How dare they bear me
Into such horror —
With no warning
I see the dawn light
touch the swans neck
And a temporary life
Is born

The summer was in our hands
We lay like fallen apples
in the grass, and as
we lay intertwined, it seemd
we, ~~like the sky~~, were endless
~~until that first duck~~
~~dove down kissd, I thought~~
~~lips were~~, we were drowning
in each other, yet neither
called ~~for~~ help, some^(how) we
had reached Camelot, the
stars came out and blessed
us, we could hear the sea
We searched each other and
found ourselves, call it love yet
it was better than that, we
made each other happen, ~~xxx~~
~~was to be second, theis earr~~

_1961._

Mermaid Theatre
December 12 1961

1961

Treasure Island 1961

Mermaid Theatre

This was the first break
I was given as an 'Actor'
by Bernard Miles. About
I had been out of work nearly
18 months, I got £15-0-0
a week.

This envelope contained the first photographs taken of Spike in the role of Ben Gunn (opposite).
He was indebted to Bernard Miles all his life. I once asked Spike, 'When does the debt get paid?'
His answer: 'Never.'

Ben Gunn, Mermaid Theatre.

Spike with his 'best mate'.

TREE MANIAC

The Tree Maniac.

Announcer: Good evening, the BBC Home Service presents the Grunes (pause) Grunes?. Grunes??? yes it quiet definately written here G-R-U-N-E-S, of course they must mean Coons - yes thats it- Coons (walks away repeating)

John Snagge (Peter) Mr Greenslade is currently being treated by Sir Charles Fees the famous Phychaitrist and used car salesman. What Greenslade meant to say was that This is the Grute Show (Pause) Grute?, now they mean Grune- L + G the Grune Show [Long Silence]

Oboe   Gives hurried tunning A to Orchestra

Snagge Bai Jove I do believe they werent quite ready - Have another try Ladies and -

Orchestra Come in too soon with signature tune.
        [Pause]

FX   Fork falls on floor

This *Goon Show* was never performed. It was found by Spike amongst some of his papers after the *Goon Show* had ended. It appeared in a book in 1987 but not in Spike's own handwriting – thought you'd like to see it.

154

Ned Seagoon: That thrilling sound of a EPNS fork hitting the ground signals the start of a mysterious mystery.

Spike (starter) On your marks - get set -

FX Starters pistol.

FX Mass of boots running away

Ned Very well I do it on my own - L+G. The landing Tree Manual

ORK Brooding - mystery chords mixed with maniacal laughter + tree chopping.

Dimbelby The Queen places the ~~Soft~~ Royal sapling in the Royal hole and with a silver shovel fills it in.

The Queen (Peter) I name this tree Copper Beech God bless its nuts and all who will assail her.

FX Feeble clapping.

Ann: Meantime - at Catford police station. a constable Oaf is at work.)

FX ~~Truncheon hitting head.~~

Constable (~~Spike~~ cockney) (beating a rubber bust of Mick Jagger.

155

Fx   Truncheon on head

Constable (Spike Cockney) Take that you hippy
          Swine

Fx.   Truncheon wallop!

Constable! earnin' on that money

Fx   Wallop

Constable singing crappy tunes!

Fx   Wallop!

Constable and me with my fine voice only
          on 18 quids a week

Fx   Wallop

Fx   Phone rings.

Constable Hello - Hello - better pick it up but
          first

Fx   Wallop

FX   Picks phone up

Constable Catford Police station.

Neddy: Heeeo this is Neddy Seagoon.
          Welsh midget. and Forester in waiting
          to the Queen!

Constable Oh, you ever seen that swine Mick
          Jagger - he gets £200,000,000 a
          minute

Fx   Wallop

Neddy   Yes - I want to report ─

Constable:	and me only £18 a week -
FX	Wallop
Neddy:	Listen constabule of old Catford. I wish to report a free vandal -
Constable	Oh - is ~~that~~ it a doggie?
Neddy	Is what a doggie.
Constable	(Barks) Bow - wow - wow - woof - Grrr - ~~thats a d~~ ?
Neddy	Whats that?
Constable	Thats a doggie!
Neddy	I thought you were a policeman
Constable	I am and its only £18 a week
FX	Wallop
Neddy	Look - you know Hernes mighty Oak ~~in~~ in Windsor Park?
Constable	Well not personally..
Neddy	Well its -
Constable	- and he's always havin' it orf with good lookin' birds -
FX	Wallop
Neddy	Look man! Hernes mighty oak has been uprooted - roots and all
Constable	- and 'ee's not even good lookin'!
FX	Wallop (continues)

The *Harry Secombe Show*. Spike wrote on the back of this photograph: ' Must be the last get together of the Goons.' But there is no date. They appeared together in 1972 for the last *Goon Show* of all at

the Camden Theatre. I think Spike got it wrong; this looks to me like a *Goon Show* rehearsal or recording.

This is just Spike doodling for future ideas.

Ann. The BBC would like to point that what they are hearing. is not typical of the police force. the Inspector has said he personally is not jealous of Mick Jagger. its that bastard Paul McCartney.

Neddy Its true. the £18 a week police were not interested folks. so I would have to go to the £10 a week police even 9 or 8! nine and eight make £17, that would only be a pound cheaper than the £18 a week understand (gibbers on)

Ann Mr Seagoon is also being treated by Sir Charles Fees.

Neddy - so money is no object - I'll just throw ~~FX this~~ this shilling on the pavement to see if theres any Scotsmen in the district.

FX Shilling on pavement. follow by approach. of two sets of boots at speed - they halt

Grytpype thynne: (breathless) m'card!

Neddy Mac Hard - ah - a real scot! - see. thynnet Moriarty financiers. and 24 hour dry cleaners.

Moriarty:. Owww

Neddy   The sound came from a shivering wreck
         wearing a wedding-tackle length vest.
         a topless bowler- and a reconditioned
         cricketers box - laying stretched on the pavement

Thynne   My partner. Count Jim 'Knackered' Moriarty
         a scion of Grade 3 Salmon has played
         the lead in several French post-cards.

Neddy: Is he dead?

Thynne   That is a trade secret - but his strength
         is unbounded - with him we can cracked
         this case open.

Neddy   So saying he cracked a case open-

FX   Case being smashed. — brilliant

Thynne   Thats just a beginning - you want
         Herons mighty oak traced

Neddy   Yes yes yes yes yes yes

Thynne   One yes would have done - you're used to
         working with the deaf or the Irish -
         Moriarty cover me with a song.

Moriarty (sings) These teeth are the teeth of a
         woman in love (continued)

Thynne   Neddy - So far our ~~enquiries~~ investigations have led
         us to this blank cheque - ~~instead~~
         it would help our enquiries - if you
         signed just here

FX   Hurried signing

Thynne   What a beautiful hand-

Mor   Yes - but a terrible signature

163

These images were in his mind when he created the written words for the *Goon Show*.

About 1954-56

He told me, 'This is how I saw them when I was writing.'

~~Thynne~~

Thynne -	Moriarty, open the Cyprus Sherry.
Fx	Pop. and pouring.
Neddy -	It, it looks like water ~~it tastes it~~
Thynne	A toast to your ~~forthcoming~~ overdraft.
~~Neddy~~	~~It tastes like water~~
Fx	Clinking glasses.
Neddy	It - it tastes like water
Thynne	Water? Theres and Old Latin adage
	Parventum - ad Hoc - nil desparandum
	Aqua frescha!
Neddy	Oh - I wish I'd met you earlier.
Thynne	So do we Neddy - say so do we
	for me Moriarty
Mor	So do we!
Fx	Terrible slap.
	Ow - mon tete!
Mor	Why do you keep hitting him
Neddy	Why? because hes there!
Thynne	Who would want to remove Herns Oak
Ann:	The first clue came from a couple living in Neasden.
Fx	Clock ticking - bed springs - ~~alarm~~ snoring. Alarm clock rings
Crun + Bannister.	Waking noises
Crun	Ah
Bannister	Ooooo

8

~~Crun. M~~

Bannister	~~Hele~~ Are you awake Henry'
Crun	I'll just look in the mirror - ---- oh. is it open eyes for awake
Bannister	Well thats how I do it!
Crun	Whats the time
Bannisle	I set the alarm for 8
Crun	Why theres only 2 of us
Bannister	There must be 6 more some where -
FX	Bong of Po.
Crun	Oh -
Bannisler	Its very dark this morning - look how dark it is out
~~Crun~~	
Crun	Thats the blinds Min
FX	Sound of door knob - and bolts ~~being~~ being with drawn.
Crun	(off mike) Oh min - there's something on the landing.
Min	It must be the cat.
Crun	No a cat could'nt do this - some ones left anOak tree on the landing - cat's cant do Oak trees
Min	Let me see - oh theres a label on it - From the Tree Maniac -
Crun	I don't remember ordering a tree from a maniac.

Min	It must be a joke.
Crun	No min - its not a joke - its definately a tree - Jokes don't have leaves on.
Min	No ~~got~~ some jokes have whiskers on.

Both talk at cross purposes (fade)

Fx	Heavy snoring.
Ann	The snoring you hear is that of the dusty fireman at Lewisham
Fx	Phone ring. Snorer wakes up
Fireman	(~~SPIKE~~) Hello Lewisham fire-brigade.
Crun	~~Hello~~ - we have a Tree on our landing.
Fireman	Thanks for telling me.
Crun	Don't go - we want help
Fireman	Well is the tree on fire?
Crun	No
Fireman	— We'll we can't come unless its on fire
Crun	Min he says he can't come unless the tree is on fire
Min	Oh I'll get a box of matches
Crun	If you come now - well have it going by the time you arrive
Fireman	Its very nice of you to put work my way

This is where I stopped

1974: The real love of his life.

1975: With Twiggy at a demonstration in Harrods against the sale of furs.

1958: Wine tasting at the Rheingold Cellar, Sydney. Spike always said he was an oenophile. Here he is trying to prove it.

SPIKE'S LETTERS

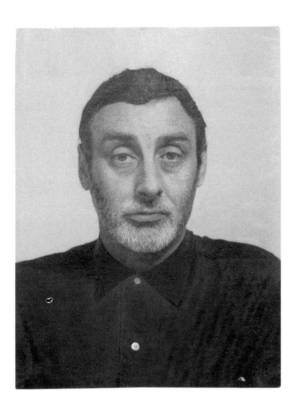

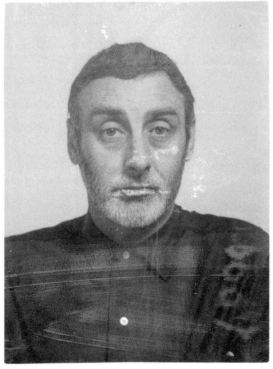

SONNRAÍ FEARSANTA—PERSONAL DES

		Sealbhóir Bearer Titulaire
Gairm ... ... Profession ... ... Profession	}	Údar Author
Áit bheireatais ... Place of birth ... Lieu de naissance	}	An Ind India
Dáta beireatais ... Date of birth ... Date de naissance	}	16 · 4 · 19 16 · 4 · 1
Áit chómhnaithe ... Residence ... ... Résidence	}	Sasan England
Aoirde ... ... Height ... ... Taille	}	5' 11 5' 11
Dath na súl ... ... Colour of eyes ... Couleur des yeux	}	Gorm Blue
Dath na gruaige ... Colour of hair ... Couleur des cheveux	}	Donn Brown
Aghaidh ... ... Face ... ... Visage	}	Ubh Cro Oval
Cómharthaí fé leith Special peculiarities Signes particuliers	}	....

Above: The passport photo he had taken for his new Irish citizen passport!

174

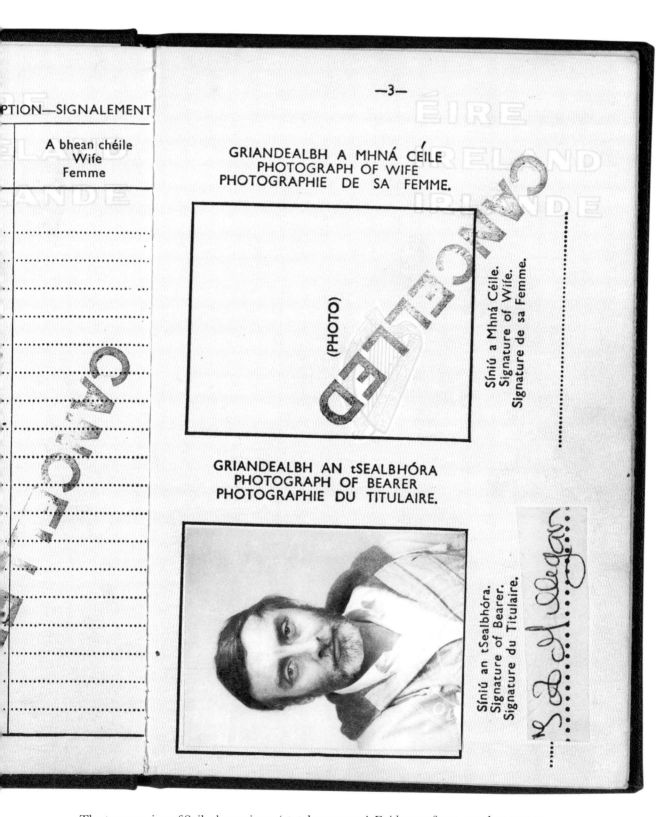

PTION—SIGNALEMENT

A bhean chéile
Wife
Femme

GRIANDEALBH A MHNÁ CÉILE
PHOTOGRAPH OF WIFE
PHOTOGRAPHIE DE SA FEMME.

(PHOTO)

Síniú a Mhná Céile.
Signature of Wife.
Signature de sa Femme.

GRIANDEALBH AN tSEALBHÓRA
PHOTOGRAPH OF BEARER
PHOTOGRAPHIE DU TITULAIRE.

Síniú an tSealbhóra.
Signature of Bearer.
Signature du Titulaire.

CANCELLED

The true version of Spike becoming a 'stateless person'. Evidence of non-stateless person.

175

Spike's parents on their way back to Australia from the Himalayas.

BY AIR MAIL   PAR AVION
AEROGRAMME

Hot Air Ballooning

AUSTRALIA   40c

WOY WOY N.S.W

TO

TO   Miss. Norma Farnes.
9 Orme Court.
Bayswater
London W.2.
England.

COUNTRY OF DESTINATION   England.
S.14.9.

From

SENDER'S NAME AND ADDRESS
Mrs. F. Mulligan
393 Orange Grove Rd.
Woy Woy N.S.W.
Australia.
Postcode 2256.

Fold flaps before moistening gum. For maximum adhesion, press down
for a few seconds. If anything is enclosed or any tape or sticker attached,

my photo was in the new paper
behind the Flag Bearer & with the
Aussie Diggers. I know he will love
that. I've quite forgotten to ask you
"How are You Mum & Jack? I do
hope all well. I keep pretty good
dear. Spike tells me he is coming
out end of June & is that right? too
I don't suppose I shall see England
this year lets see anyway Des Wadia
Michael & Mum all send their love.

...on your nice letter by by.   affectionate
                                  Grandma

My Dearest Norma.

XXXXXXX
love to Tanis mum & Jack
You must be thinking I've
forgotten all about you. My dear you
know I could never do that you are
my adopted daughter, but I have
had a lot of official functions thrust
on me for the last six weeks or so.
        You know Spike was doing the
promotion commercial for our Lovely
new Shopping Complex in my my.
I the Lord Mayor of Gospel City
roped me in to carry out the
opening ceremony & cut the Ribbon
to open the "Complex". 30,000 people
flocked through the doors as soon
as it opened. I was feted and
photos taken with the Mayor
& Directors of the Stores (45 Shops)
inside. All top Class. I am just
getting ready the photos etc to
send to my dear Spike. I have
been very worried (don't tell him this)
about his eyes. Are they really
getting better Norma. It is awful
when one is so far away. I know
if I was there I could not do much & the Army.
By the way, I was in the Army's
Annual March with the digger's
& my our Force girl pals we all
meet every Year. I wear dads
7 medals and away I go. I am
sending Spike that photo as
well as soon as I get it.

My dearest Norma,

You must be thinking I've forgotten all about you. My dear you know I could never do that you are my adopted daughter, but I have had a lot of official functions thrust on me for the last six weeks or so.

You know Spike was doing the promotion commercial for our <u>lovely</u> new Shopping Complex in Woy Woy. & the Lord Mayor of Gosford City roped me in to carry out the opening ceremony and cut the Ribbon to open the Complex. <u>30,000</u> people flocked through the doors as soon as it opened. I was feted and photos taken with the Mayor, and Directors of the stores (45 shops) inside, all top class. I am just getting ready the photos etc to send to my dear Spike. I have been <u>very</u> <u>worried</u> (don't tell him tho' about his eyes. Are they really getting better Norma. It is awful when one is so far away. I know I could not do much if I was there By the way, I went in the <u>ANZAC</u> annual march with the diggers & my Air Force girl pals We all meet every year. I wear dads 7 medals and away I go. I am sending Spike that photo as well as soon as I get it. My photo was in the newspaper behind the Flag Bearer & with the Aussie Diggers. I know he will <u>love</u> that. Ive quite forgotten to ask you How are you mum and Jack? I do hope all well. I keep pretty good dear. Spike tells me he is coming out end of June? is that right so I dont suppose I shall see England this year. Lets see anyway. Des Nadia Michael & Mum all send their love.

I'll write sooner darling. Thanks for your nice letter by by. Affectionately

Grandma

X X X X X X

How did the wedding go??

Love to Tanis Mum & Jack.

Now you know where Spike got it from: a truly formidable woman whom I loved.

Spike performing in *Idiots' Weekly* for ABC Sydney.

HARRODS
HARRODS LTD
KNIGHTSBRIDGE
LONDON SW1

Telephone: SLOane 1234

SPIKE MILLIGAN ESQ.
9 ORME COURT,
LONDON W 2.

YOUR PERSONAL
ACCOUNT NUMBER

4527326
19/12/65

YOU MAY PAY YOUR
ACCOUNT THROUGH
ANY BANK BY USING
THE CREDIT TRANSFER
OVERLEAF. IF PAYING
DIRECT, PLEASE RE-
TURN THE TOP PART
OF THIS STATEMENT.

PAYMENTS AND CREDITS MADE
AFTER THIS DATE WILL BE
SHOWN ON THE NEXT STATEMENT.

RECEIPTS FOR CHEQUES
WILL BE SENT ON
REQUEST ONLY.

Cash £50/0/0. 6/1/66

DETACH HERE

DATE	DESCRIPTION	PURCHASES	CASH & CREDITS	REF. No.	FOR YOUR OWN NOTES
8 DEC	BALANCE FROM NOV CASH	406. 7.1	50. 0.0	028	

356. 7.1	
AMOUNT TO BE PAID	AMOUNT IN CREDIT

HARRODS
HARRODS LTD.
KNIGHTSBRIDGE
LONDON SW1
Telephone: SLOane 1234

Spike's logic: Harrods took two years to do the job; he will take two years to pay.

HARRODS
HARRODS LTD

KNIGHTSBRIDGE
LONDON SW1

Telephone Sloane 1234   Telegrams "Harrods London, Telex."

Miss Alice Bolton
Secretary to
Spike Milligan Esq
9 Orme Court
W.2

24 Jan 66

③

Dear Madam

re Spike Milligan Account

      We enclose a further statement of
account compiled to the 19th December from which
after allowing your payment of £50.0.0d received
on the 6th January, leaves an outstanding balance
of £306.7.1d.

      As stated in our letter of the 16th
December, our terms of credit are for full
settlement of accounts as rendered. We are
therefore unable to agree to accept settlement
of the enclosed account by instalments of
£50.0.0d.

      The Company's Annual Audit falls
due on the 31st January and we must ask for a
cheque in full settlement before that date.

                      Yours faithfully
                      Harrods Ltd

                      H T Dugdale
                      Accounts Dept

Ref: 4527326/48

9 Orme Court,
London, W.2.

26th January 1966

SM/AJB

the Chairman,
Harrods Ltd.,
Knightsbridge,
London, S.W.1.

Dear Sir,

    I am being badgered into paying the enclosed bill.
I decided to pay this bill at the same rate at which
Harrods did the job, overall it took two years from the
first phone call until the final completion of the job
during which time I spent no less than 24 of my working
hours attending workmen on the site who had come with
insufficient instructions and also left all their
paraphernalia in the front garden after the job was
finished.

    No I will pay this bill in the way I think fit
and if you wish to take me to court I have a complete
analysis of the work and I will be only too glad to
let the press know how the work was done.

                    Yours faithfully,

                    SPIKE MILLIGAN
                    ━━━━━━━━━━━━━━━

c.c. Louis Tarlo*

* His solicitor.

HARRODS
HARRODS LTD

KNIGHTSBRIDGE
LONDON SW1

RHH/FEM

Telephone Sloane 1234 Telegrams"Everything Harrods London"

28th January, 1966

S. Milligan Esq.,
9, Orme Court,
London W.2.

Dear Sir,

I beg to acknowledge your letter of
26th January, 1966, on behalf of the Chairman, and
in his absence from this office to-day your letter has
been passed to the Managing Director for his personal
attention.

Yours faithfully,

Cdr.Sir Robert Hobart, Bt. R.N.
Personal Assistant to The Lord Fraser
of Allander

File »

HARRODS LTD

KNIGHTSBRIDGE

LONDON SW1

Telephone Sloane 1234 Telegrams"Everything Harrods London"

BY APPOINTMENT
TO HER MAJESTY THE QUEEN
SUPPLIERS OF CHINA, GLASS
AND FANCY GOODS

BY APPOINTMENT
SUPPLIERS OF CHINA, GLASS
AND FANCY GOODS TO
H.M. QUEEN ELIZABETH THE QUEEN MOTHER

Your ref: SM/AJB

17th February, 1966

S. Milligan, Esq.,
9 Orme Court,
London, W.2.

Dear Sir,

    I have been asked by the Managing Director to investigate the complaints contained in your letter of the 26th January and in consequence I have seen Mr. Valentine the Manager of our Building and Decorating Department and obtained his report.

    I am told the facts are as follows:-

Date of enquiry 10th March 1965
A representative called on the 19th March 1965
Our estimate FL.224 is dated 30th March 1965
Order was issued on the 3rd April 1965
The last entry in cost book regarding labour is week
                           ending 15th August 1965

    It would therefore appear that the job covered a period of about $4\frac{1}{2}$ months including additional work to estimate. I understand the small amount of plant required for the work was stacked in the front garden and removed in early July when no longer needed. It would seem that the work was completed in a very much shorter period than as stated in your letter and I am afraid we are not prepared to accept settlement of your account by instalments and I trust that after further consideration you will be good enough to let us have your cheque in settlement without further delay.

                Yours faithfully,

                L. STUART
                Credit Manager

LS/CB
45 273 26

9 Orme Court,
London, W.2.

18th February 1966.

SM/SC/AJB

Mr. L. Stewart,
Credit Manager,
Harrods Ltd.,
Knightsbridge,
London, S.W.3.

Dear Sir,

      The facts that you quote are
the only facts you have. If you want to hear
the real facts, take me to court, I would love
to unfold the story very much, because I have
really had a bellyful of the customer always
being wrong. So go ahead, I'll see you in court.

      Yours faithfully,

HARRODS

HARRODS LTD

KNIGHTSBRIDGE
LONDON SW1

Telephone Sloane 1234   Telegrams " Harrods London Telex "

30 Mar 66

S Milligan Esq
9 Orme Court
W.2

Dear Sir

Thank you for your recent payment of £50.0.0d on account.

However, as stated in our letter of the 17th February, we are not prepared to accept settlement of your account by instalments and we must ask you, therefore, to let us have, by return, your cheque for £264.13.1d, as shown on the enclosed statement, to clear the balance still outstanding.

Failing receipt of your cheque, we will be reluctantly compelled to pass the matter to the Company's Solicitors for their attention.

Yours faithfully
Harrods Ltd

H J Dugdale
Accounts Dept

Ref: 4527326/48

9 Orme Court,
London, W.2.

31st March 1966.

Your Ref. 4527326/48

Our Ref. SM/AJB

H.J. Dugdale Esq.,
Accounts Department,
Harrods Ltd.,
Knightsbridge,
London, S.W.1.

Dear Sir,

By all means then pass it to
your Company solicitors for their
attention, I will instruct my solicitor
likewise.   I will look forward to this
clash with utter and complete joy.   I
think my revelations will enlighten both
you and the public in Court.

Yours faithfully,

9 Orme Court,
LONDON. W. 2.

Tel. PAR. 2768.

2nd June, 1967

The London Nameplate Manufacturing Co. Ltd.,
Zylo Works,
BRIGHTON, 7.

For the attention of:- Mr. Oliver.

Dear Mr. Oliver,

Further to our telephone conversation of yesterday afternoon, I should like to confirm that I require one brass plate, with the wording as follows:-

IN MEMORY OF A TULIP RALLY BADGE WON BY
BILL WARD, AND STOLEN BY SPIKE MILLIGAN
WHO WAS SUDDENLY TAKEN DRUNK.
MAY GOD HAVE MERCY ON HIS SOUL.

I should be grateful if you could make the plate with a small hole in each corner for screws, (enclosed is a sample).

I should like the same size as the previous two you have made for us 5" x 2½".

If you have any problems, please don't hesitate to get in touch with me.

I should be grateful if you could het me know when I could expect delivery.

Sincerely,

Norma Farnes
Assistant to Spike Milligan.

His saving grace was his conscience – never more so than here.

393 Orange Grove Road   Friday 27 Sept. 1968.

    Woy Woy

    N.S.W.

Hello Darling clever posh bird,

                    Sorry I have'nt written you a letter of any length,

but life out here is getting bloody hectic, I'm now getting mail to answer

and have no secretary, i.e. I've been up since 8, and as yet I have'nt started

work on any thing I want to do , its all fan letters. letters from charities,

from people who say ' You remember me I met you in 1934 etc etc', I have to sign

forms for any work I do and post them all my self, this means a journey of 2

miles to Woy Woy Post office , I have to cut out write ups, read the papers to

find out whats going on in the world. answer the phone, its now 12 O'clock,

and I'm still answerijg letters. Nothing to report that desperately urgent,

I'm doing occassional work to earn money , so far its reached the astronomical

sum of about £,1000, for about two months, I'm trying to avoid drawing money

from England because since devaluation the rate of exchange is unfavourable,

I think I will be able to return the £1,000 to Coutts untouched, it was just

a standby im case I bought a piece of land (I'm still looking). I did a Job for

Channel 7 in Melbourne 'A Guy called Athol' its a show with one of thr original

Seekers (They've disbanded) , I got them to pay for my mother to xomexaxzx go as

well, we went on the Souther Aurora, a luxury air conditioned train, with a

bar, Dining room, and a sleeping berth which folds into a comfy arm chair, built

in are wash basin tpilet etc. Did the show, saw interest points, Captain Cooks

Cottage, (Transported from England) , Cottage (later used as the State of Victori

-as first Goverment House) of Charles La Trobe, first Govenor General of

of Victoria, it was prefabribcated in England and transported to Australia

in 1839. (Did you get the envelope of flower petals from our garden? Hope

so.) On the return journey we came back in daylight, and saw the countless

rolling acres of sheep farms, passed the Famous Glen Rowan Hotel where Ned Kelly

and his gang(Rebel Irish Hooray!) fought their last battle with the State Troopers.

Bill Kerr will tell you all about it, talking of him '(The bloody thief, I learned

that the act he used to do 'I've only got four minutes' was stolen from an old

Australian comic, and thats why he did'nt ever c ome back to Australia, he is

a scoundrel. We got home last night at about 10.30 at night, mum was

whacked, it was good to get back to the clean air of the country and sea.

As always, telling me how hard he's working and the promise of his poetry book being finished (twice), to keep me quiet.

191

September 1977: Me in front of all the files. The missing files would be the ones he was working on.

So I'm back at the 'desk' writing, always bloody writing. Will you send the
enclosed newscutting to Bill Kerr. Tell him I've been thru Wagga Wagga,
and they say they're waitinf forX him to get back half their bloody homes
from him , tell him I met the small man from Warren Laytona and Sparks who sent
Bill regards. Let me know how much my Mrs has sunk me for in money, just so I
know. Don't forget to check with my letter about the odds and ends I want
the painters to observe when finishing, i.e. seeing that all the sash windows
are free and eased to allow them to be moved up and down . When they sand the
floor, ask them to use a vacum sander, its one th t sucks up the dirt as it
sands, after they've sanded, get Dorothy to 'Feather dust the walls to clean
off any deposits, you may not be able to see them but they are there.
Sorry you're bored, I feel helpless at the moment, all I can do is to try
and finish the book before I return. I have decided that it will have to be a
Trilogy, Part One From Joining the Army to going Overseas. 2) From going into
action to the end of the War. Frmmx 3) from the end of th4 War to Demob.
Each book being thirty thousand words. I think thats what I'll do. I think.
No more news. When I return I'll start writing the TV Show, I'd like it to be
good. Phone Carol Jonas at Ronnie Scotts, tell her I love her and I think
of her.(Must keep my birds happy) I don't know what to think about the
Broadway 'Oblomov' I don't seem to be able to get excited about it, that
might be a good thing. Give my love to our Posh Switch Board girl Kathy,
tell her I love her . Have you got rid of all the surplus GPO Phones if not
do so, also check all the other numerous GPO Lines that go up the
back stairs and make 'em take out the dud ones, and label the ones in use
with what they are. Can you get the Door Bells Mamdmdî Mended, get the front
porch floor cleaned and re polished. I'll keep sweating it out out here.
Phone me a couple of times a week, more of ness.

                    Love to all (Le Barr included)
                         Spike

WED 3 Oct.

Dear Fat posh dolly bird,

Business. 1) Don't want to do The Commuter'
its a Sellers cast off, I dont like secon hand clothes. Forget it.
2) If Phillip has nothing to do. Will he put all Press cuttings in order in

my Press Books in my Private Cupboard on Landing.

3) Have you Paid Jack Hobbs for the printing of my dads 4 Books. If not do so.

4) Do Mermaid have a break down of how the finances of the Theatre work ?

Like what salaries, what profits in Resturant, in other words a complete

picture of Mermaids financial structure.

5) OK about Mermaid re election.

6. BARRY Green EMI. I wash my hands of all anything to do with the LP Cover,

after they behaved so abominiably last time including loosing my design, Sod

'em.

7) If they (EMI) want photos of Green tell them we are not a photoagency for the

Goon Show, the BBC are , like wise try Secombe and Sellers who do buggerall

to put these records out, and collect money for it. No Photos tell them, all

gone.

8 Gold Frame for my painting of coloured church windows, for Hattie Jaques.

N.B. Make sure they Insure the paintings, each one is worth £ 150.

9+) When When When, is D Dobson printing the Bed Sit ? Hes had it over

a year, and I keep getting letters about where people can get it. Will he

please put it on the production line. Tell him this One year to get out

a book is a bit slow by other firms standards,

10 Have BBC Sent Beachcomber Film yet URGENT. I must know while Im out here.

So I can do something to make them get a move on. FLASH. I've jsut phoned

Davic Stone of ABC out here, he has asked them for it, and it as yet has'nt

arrived, will you ask them wahts the hold up ? PLEASE, GET SOME SENSE FROM THEM.

Tell BBC I'm hanging on out here to see the print they send to view it with

the ABC.

11 Milliganimals, did you say its out in October ? Well if it is as Dobson to send

me a copy, I could plug it out here,. In a rush to Past this
Phone me Love Spike

194

Dear Norma + Tams —

Not much time - hectic - one
nighters - sleep in suit case -
Did great at Twin Towns - Sell out
at Myella - Sell out Adelaide (1,500)
Sold out at Renmark (to-nyght) sold
out at Adelaide tomorrow (1,500) -
But no life as such travel - perform -
- Sleep - but its Barnstorming -
Show Biz - going great - very hard
to phone you as I write - its
11.20 am here but 10 to 3 in the
morning UK - I leave here at 3
in afternoon - arrive Renmark 6 -
no phone possible as its 9 am -
I'm on at 7.30 - 11.30 your time

9 Orme Court,
LONDON. W. 2.

28th January, 1969

The Caxton Nameplate Co. Limited,
Kew Green,
Kew,
SURREY.

Dear Sirs,

I wonder if you could make for me, three small brass
plates, with the following inscriptions.

1)   This door was taken from 54 Hunter Street, London.
      the childhood home of J. Ruskin.

2)   This fireplace was saved from 54 Hunter Street,
      London. the childhood home of J. Ruskin.

3)   This console and mirror was taken from Brent Lodge,
      Finchley, before destruction by a Philistine Local
      Council.

The size should be 5" long by 2" wide, with screw holes
at each of the four corners.

Perhaps you could let me know, as soon as possible, if you
can do this for me.

                              Sincerely,

                              Spike Milligan.

The preservation Milligan. They were given to Bernard Miles for the Mermaid Theatre Museum.

Wildlife

9 Orme Court,
LONDON. W. 2.

Tel. PAR 2768

18th March, 1968

Peter Scott Esq.,
Wildfowl Trust,
Slimbridge,
GLOUCESTER.

Dear Peter,

I am writing to you about the condition, during the mating season
of Mallards in Hyde Park, Kensington Park and St. James's Park.

The females are taking a terrible thrashing to the point of death
which I have seen myself.

Having made a quick tour round the parks on Sunday the females are
outnumbered 10-1, 5-1, and 3-1.   <u>Something has to be done.</u>

The solution is very simple, to save gross maltreatment of the
females, the males have got to be thinned out by shooting. The
second, which would be much more difficult, would be trapping
them at night by hand, taking them to distant parts of the
country and releasing them which, of course, is out of the **questi**
question.

The doddering Ministry of Public Buildings and Works, who should
really be solving the **problem** are doing what most of the English
are doing these days, flapping their hands and saying 'we can't
do anything'.

So I am writing to you to ask for your help. I am writing
around to other organisations, the R.S.P.C.A. my local M.P. and
R.S.P.B.

The killings need not be useless, the ducks could be given to
the Chelsea Pensioners who I am sure would enjoy eating them.

Do you know any good Wildfowlers who could shoot these, and are
willing to come to London in the early hours of the morning
before the parks are opened, and start thinning the males out.

Tons of love, keep fighting.

Spike Milligan

Conservationist.

197

9 Orme Court,
London, W.2.

13th March 1973

The Editor,
U.A.C.T.A. Magazine,
52 High Street,
Fordingbridge,
Hants.

Dear Vigilantes,

Just a line to ask you to bear in mind the precarious
state of the whale. As you know, there has been no complete
ban on whaling and some countries are still taking the most
terrible toll of this magnificent and irresistible leviathan
of the deep. I notice on page 4 of the current magazine that
we are appealing for people to take specially printed postcards
which can be forwarded to the Secretary of State and/or their
Member of Parliament. I think whole schools ought to take
them and send them en masse to our gentlement in parliament.

I want to thank you again for the efforts you are making,
also to congratulate Joey Gregg and Trudi Harrison for winning
the Dr. Albert Schweitzer Award. It makes me feel very good
to know that young people are showing the way to a world of
almost blind adults.

Love, Light and Peace,

Spike Milligan

9, Orme Court,
LONDON, W. 2.

1st June 1971.

The Lady who answers the 'phone
at 580-4034
Animals' Vigilantes,
51, Harley Street,
London, W1N 1DD

Dear Madam,

I am the impossible person who actually dared to
ask you your name the other day. I find it almost
unbelieveable to think that your parents took the loving
care to baptize you as a child and you ignore that because
you have become over bureaucrasized. The world that
George Orwell predicted was opened up to me when you said
the immortal lines "I am only allowed to give names of
people of those in authority".

Supposing I would not give my name, how would we
ever communicate? Cogitate on that dear nameless lady.

Sincerely,

Spike Milligan.

Compassion for the animals – but none for the 'nameless lady'.

With the approach of Christmas, the year 1975 draws to ~~and~~ a close - in retrospect was it a better world for animals? I'd love to say yes, but the answer is no. The horrible use of Beagles by ICI was one reminder of the debased levels at which our laughingly called 'civilization' works at. as I write this I read of more awful experiments at Cambridge University using kittens, the import of animals by air continues, with absolutely <u>no</u> gorantee of their safety ~~either~~ by the Air-lines, the dealers or our own dear Minister of.... Fred Peart, this month 2,000 little birds were delivered dead at London Airport - and what is degradingly immoral is the Air Lines won't reveal the names of the dealers; I won't depress you further with these ~~acts of~~ monsterous acts by man, ws Just to remind you that the need to fight ~~this~~ animal cruelty is even more important than ever, even when a law <u>is</u> put forward ie The anti hare coursing Bill

it fails to get thru past Parliament! And thats
the heart of our democratic life style –
remember, there are Members of Parliament
who are MONSTERS, when time comes to
vote ask them their views on Bloodsports
– etc, and vote accordingly. Now, happier
things, I want all children and their families
to have a HAPPY one, it does.int have to be
an expensive one – just one with love
in the family – and love for nature and
humanity. I put nature first, because
without it there would be no mankind,
Think of the words of that very nice
man Jesus, all he preached was love
and truth towards all, if only those words
would get thru to the Fox Hunters –
the Veal Calf breeders – the Vivisectionists –
those awful men who take baby monkeys
away from their mothers just to see
what happens – we can only hope and
pray that one day . . . . I will spend
any Christmas with any family – and after
our Christmas Dinner – we will drink
a toast to all of you from us,
Love light and Peace
from Spike

With the approach of Christmas, the year 1975 draws to a close
in retrospect was it a better world for animals? I'd love to
say yes, but the answer is no.   The horrible use of Beagles
by I.C.I. was one reminder of the debased levels at which our
laughingly called "civilisation" works at, as I write this I
read of more awful experiments at Cambridge University using
kittens, the import of animals by air continues, with absolutely
no guarantee of their safety either by the Airlines, the dealers
or our own Minister of Agriculture, Fisheries and Food, Fred Peart,
this month 2,000 little birds were delivered dead at London
Airport - and what is degradingly immoral is, the Airlines
won't reveal the names of the dealers; I won't depress you
further with these monstrous acts by man, it's just to remind
you that the need to fight animal cruelty is even more important
than ever, even when a law is put forward, i.e. The Anti Hare
Coursing Bill, it fails to get through Parliament.   And, that's
the heart of our democratic life style - remember, there are
Members of Parliament who are MONSTERS, when time comes to vote,
ask them their views on Bloodsports, etc. and vote accordingly.

Now, happier things, I want all children and their families
to have a HAPPY one, it doesn't have to be an expensive one -
just one with love in the family - and love for nature and
humanity.   I put nature first, because without it, there would
be no mankind.

/Contd...

Think of the words of that very nice man Jesus, all
he preached was love and truth towards all, if only those
words w uld get through to the Foxhunters - the Veal Calf
breeders - the Vivisectionists - those awful men who take
baby monkies away from their mothers, just to see what happens -
we can only hope and pray that one day ....
I will spend my Christmas with my family, and after our
Christmas dinner - we will drink a toast to all of you from
us.

                              Love, light and peace,

20 November 1978

Animals' Vigilantes
James Mason House
24 Salisbury Street
Fordingbridge SP6 1AF

Dear Friends

I thought I would drop a message of Christmas good cheer to you
all and try and encourage you in our unending fight for the
world of animals.

I am sure you must have noticed the very very gradual change
that is taking place in the attitue towards animals among those
people at the top that are normally indifferent to animal
suffering. The case in question was the success of animal
lovers preventing the slaughter of 5,000 seals, as you know the
number was reduced to 2,000. Even that is horrible but at
least 3,000 seals are alive today because of people like
ourselves, so we should feel well pleased that our efforts are
showing some small measures of reward around the world.

Of course we must not let up for one moment because waiting to
rush in at the least weakness are those people who thrive on
using animals for profit. Even as I write you know full well
that veal calves are being kept in little pens, battery hens in
cooped up circumstances, all of which are totally abnormal and
unnecessary, but apropro these creatures that none of our members
should ever eat veal or take eggs from battery hens. Of course
I am sure that none of you do.

.../

Anyhow Christmas is coming and I want you all to have as good
a time as possible and remember that on that far distant
Christmas when the Saviour was born he chose to have around
him a cow, a donkey and a sheep. I think somehow there is
a message in that.
A Very Merry Christmas to you all and keep fighting.

Love, Light and Peace

Spike Milligan

```
                                    9 Orme Court,
                                    LONDON. W. 2.

                                    21st September, 1976


The Editor,
Daily Mail,
Fleet Street,
LONDON. E.C.4.

Sir,

Re Mr. Whiteley's quote "there must be an end to immigration",
If he is saying they are worried about the number of immigrants,
then is worry has come too late in the day to curb any increase.

I mean they are now procreating their own species in this country,
so they come in via the womb.

It's too late, it's much too late to do anything about England
maintaining an Eglish character.  We now have to become a Multi-
racial society, and put up with it, so any thought of curbing
immigration is just an anachronism;  it's too late they are already
here.

I am not a racialist, I am only commenting on the absurdity of
the lack of logic among some politicians.


                                    Sincerely,




                                    Spike Milligan.
```

This is the sort of thing that got Spike branded as a racist – which he definitely was not. He was concerned about the dangers of unfettered immigration changing the English character – in 1976!

9 Orme Court
LONDON W2

1 February 1978

The Editor
The Guardian
119 Farringdon Rd
LONDON EC1

Dear Sir

Regarding the current racial furor.
God knows, I am an apostle of freedom, freedom for all I
say, but there does come a point when one becomes
suspicious as to the possibilities that can occur in
a democracy if immigration is allowed to go unchecked.
A prime example is Fiji where the native Fijians are
now outnumbered by Asians. Democractically this means
that the Asians should really now hold political power
in the country and I know from personal experience that
the Fijians are violently against this. Is it this
which possibly makes lots of the native English worried
about the future of immigration? I think yes, but in
no way can these people be called racialists.
I would like readers reactions to this.

                              Yours

                              Spike Milligan

P.S. No "you are a racial bastard" letters please

Twenty-eight years later: how perspicacious and far-sighted – still going unchecked.

9 Orme Court
LONDON W2

10 May 1978

The Editor
The Guardian
119 Farringdon Road
LONDON EC1

Dear Sir

When Maria Colwell was killed by her father there was a
great investigation into the injustice of her death.
Recommendations were made and the laws appertaining to
child welfare "tightened up". Yet I read (the Guardian
9 May) in 1975 Richard Fraser was admitted to hospital
with 30 burns caused by cigarettes. How then in God's
name was the child still in the "care" of the same parents
in 1978?
No matter what any indignant Doctor, Welfare Worker,
Policeman, neighbours, etc say, somewhere there is a
person, if not persons, whose reactions to the cigarette
burnings must have been tantamount to inertia. How long
must a system exist when it is possible for a child to be
gradually tortured and finally killed over a period of
YEARS? If there was something rotten in the State of
Denmark then there is something putrid in the Welfare
State of England.

Yours faithfully

Spike Milligan

In answer to his question, posed in 1978: yes, the system still exists, but is much worse.

Maria Cowell

Good night Maria,
~~Th~~ They have just changed you
from one darkness to another

You left behind
the eternal promise of light,
of a seedlings
left in cruel adult-frosts.

When spring comes
how many will miss your flower?
if you had grown
in my garden
We could have won
prizes together.

Good bye Maria

Your gardners
are still alive

In a Taxi to some
panther place
march 75

A poem he wrote for Maria Colwell.

Spike gave me this photo. 'Shame I didn't have his mind.' 'Einstein, I presume,' I said.

```
                                        9 Orme Court,
                                        LONDON. W. 2.

                                        27th February, 1978


The Editor,
Guardian,
119 Farringdon Road,
LONDON. EC1R. 3ER.



Sir,

Reference the sex debate on Donald Duck.  Fabian Acker
suggests that there is no visible evidence of Donald
Duck's male potential.   May I point out to Mr. Acker
that male ducks "don't let it all hang out".  When needs be
Donald most certainly could consummate the marriage with
Daisy - Up-sa-daisey.


                         Sincerely,




                         Spike Milligan.
```

This was the Milligan I loved.

Dear Sir,

How long do we have to suffer authors who seek fame by ~~rewriting history~~. ~~Sensationalism~~ sensationalism? 'Laurence made up rape story' (Sun Times. 12 June) Why stop there, why not go the whole absurd hog, ie There was no such ~~person~~ as T E Lawrence - it was in fact D.H Lawrence in disguise - ~~who in fact~~. When T E Lawrence was supposed to be in Derra, it was not him, because ~~I can prove~~ he was in fact playing second violin in Mrs Cruels Gipsy Trio at the ~~Fenton~~ Fontana Tea Rooms in Brighton. Likewise he never wrote the Seven Pillars of Wisdom, ~~he only wrote~~ that was his Aunt, ~~Ely Druet Mrs~~ ~~Therma~~ ~~Sarah~~ Edith Lawrence, a lesbian History teacher at ~~Red~~ Rhodean. The man claiming to be Aircraftsman Shaw was in fact Capt Ball V.C. ~~As believed~~ ~~killed in~~ shot down over France; who resigned to avoid paying for his damaged aircraft. ~~in fact he crashed~~ ~~lost his memory and was told he was Shaw by a~~ ~~an Army Psychiatrist, was was~~ into an RAF recruiting depot, ~~lost his memory,~~ The man killed on a motorbike was also not Lawrence - no, it was Tom Mountain a failed ~~writerist~~ mime artist, disguised himself as Lawrence hoping to get some publicity - he did - in the Obituary Columns. The real T E Lawrence went on to change his name to ~~Lee~~ Harvey Oswald, the rest is history - except that the man who killed him was not Jack Ruby - it was Ronald Biggs who did the million pound train robbery to try and bribe Lord Goodman to defend him, to-day the Ronald Biggs in South America is only a plant, the real DH Lawrence to-day lives in retirement in Ditchling and collects the snails eggs,.

Sincerely ~

Spike Milligan

PS oh yes ! I forgot ! wow ! Hitler by David Irving ! Of course that Hitler didn't kill 6,000,000 Jews, impossible, because Hitler in fact was a life sized wooden dummy (~~made from wood chopped by the Kaiser~~) made by Nancy Mitford as a present for Martin Bormann, who used the dummy to blame for his own perverse sado-sexual desires. Ie: killing naked Jews? Who then committed suicide in the Bunker? It was a woman transvestite (impressionist) Maria Schmells, who was standing in for the dummy while it was being treated for dry-rot, she was playing Irish Roulette (same as Russian only ~~all the chambers are~~ there's a bullet in every chamber) with Eva Braun, when an accident occurs.

SM

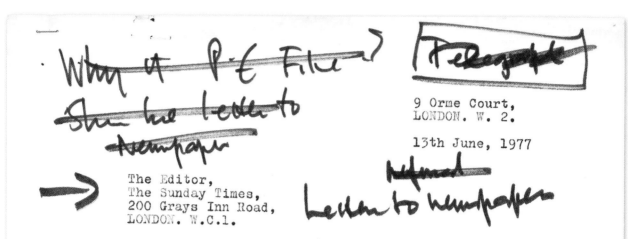

Why it P.E File?

Letter to newspaper

Telegraph

9 Orme Court,
LONDON. W. 2.

13th June, 1977

The Editor,
The Sunday Times,
200 Grays Inn Road,
LONDON. W.C.1.

Letter to newspaper

Dear Sir,

How long do we have to suffer authors who seek fame by
sensationalism?   Lawrence made up rape story (Sunday
Times 12th June), why stop there, why not go the whole
absurd hog, i.e. there was no such person as T.E. Lawrence -
it was, in fact, D.H. Lawrence in disguise - when T.E.
Lawrence was <u>supposed</u> to be in Derra, it was not him,
because he was, in fact, playing second violin in Mrs.
Cruels Gipsey Trio at the Fontana Tea Rooms in Brighton.
Likewise, he never wrote the Seven Pillars of Wisdom, that
was his Aunt, Theresa Edith Lawrence, a Lesbian History
Teacher at Roedean.   The man claiming to be Aircraftsman
Shaw was, in fact, Capt. Ball, V.C., believed shot down
over France, who rejoined to avoid paying for his damaged
aircraft.   The man killed on a motorbike was also not
Lawrence - no, it was Tom Mountain a failed mime artist,
disguised himself as Lawrence, hoping to get some
publicity - he did - in the Obituary Columns.
The real T.E. Lawrence went on to change his name to Lee
Harvey Oswald, the rest is history - except that the man
who killed him was not Jack Ruby - it was Ronald Biggs
who did the million pound train robbery to try and bribe
Lord Goodman to defend him, today the Ronald Biggs in

/Contd..

What would he have said about *The Da Vinci Code*?

South America is only a plant, the real D.H. Lawrence today lives in retirement in Ditchling and collects snails eggs.

Sincerely,

Spike Milligan.

P.S.   Oh yes! I forgot - Wow! Hitler by David Irving! Of course, Hitler didn't kill 6,000,000 Jews, impossible, because Hitler, in fact, was a life sized wooden dummy made by Nancy Mitford as a present for Martin Bormann, who used the dummy to blame for his own perverse sado-sexual desires, i.e. killing naked Jews.   Who then committed suicide in the Bunker?   It was a woman transvestite impressionist, Maria Schmells, who was standing in for the dummy while it was being treated for dry rot, she was playing Irish Roulette (same as Russian only there's a bullett in every chamber) with Iva Bruan, when an accident occurs.

S.M.

9 Orme Court,
LONDON. W. 2.

6th October, 1980

Lord Miles,
Mermaid Theatre,
Puddle Dock,
Blackfriars,
LONDON. E.C.4.

I am sorry I will be cruising somewhere in the Balearics
on that day, but give my love to those swines who are making
money by sitting at the telephone letting other people
squander theirs.   Tell them that I hope during the
proceedings, Jesus does not repeat his entry, and do
what he did to the money lenders.

I wonder what Ladbrokes were quoting when Jesus was on the
Cross - "Would he go at 2-00 p.m. 3-00 p.m. or 4-00 p.m."
or would the thieves each side of him (who were 100 to 1
on) become the favourites.

The golden sand of time is running, and I haven't seen you
for nearly two years. Yet we love each other; why then
is this pernicious system in charge of us, and not the
reverse?

My love to Lady Miles.

Love, light and peace,

Spike Milligan.

P.S. I notice that your name hasn't gone metric yet.

A letter to a friend. 'The men in suits are trying to get rid of him', Spike prophesied. And they did.

SAME LETTER SENT TO:

FINANCIAL TIMES.
THE STAGE.

9 Orme Court,
LONDON. W. 2.

15th January, 1982

The Editor,
The Times,
200 Grays Inn Road,
LONDON. WC1. X8. EZ.

Dear Sir,

Many people from the entertainment world will be depressed
at the forced resignation (for forced it was) of Sir Lew
Grade.
It was Lew and Leslie Grade's agency which helped hundreds
of us during the post war variety years, but for them it
would not have existed.   They only left it when they
realised television was the coming thing.
O.K. so "Raise the Titanic" lost a lot of money. I ask
you what Company doesn't.   What about British Leyland,
at least Sir Lew never went cap in hand begging for money,
it was always on a business basis.   What other Chairman
would you find at his desk at 6-00 and 7-00 in the morning?
Of course, he gave a large golden handshake, he was a big
man, he still is a big man.
Holmes A'Court has got the Company, not because he is
interested in show business, but because he is nothing
more than a business magnate.
I am appalled at the short memories of the world of
finance.
This man could have made it again and again if he was
just given breathing space.

Sincerely,

Spike Milligan.

Defending a friend.

9 Orme Court,
LONDON. W. 2.

30th March, 1982

Lord Carrington, KC., MG., MC.,
Secretary of State for the
                    Foreign & Commonwealth Office,
King Charles Street,
LONDON. S.W.1.

Dear Lord Carrington,

Just to congratulate you and your Foreign Office
on it's 200th Anniversary.
Thought you would like one from a clown.

Love, light and peace,

Spike Milligan.

He liked Lord Carrington and it shows.

9 Orme Court,
LONDON. W. 2.

12th March, 1984

Paul Getty Jnr. Esq.,
Tudor House,
16 Cheyne Walk,
LONDON. S.W.3.

My dear Paul,

Your kindness baffles me; we live in a society of human
beings whose indifference can only be likened to a
stagnant mill pond, where there is no sign of life above
or below the water.

First of all these gifts of wine; I have a deep suspicion
that you are trying to wean me on to high class expensive
wines, so when I am finally hooked and incapable of buying
these quality clarets, and I am trying to get a fix on
cheap Sainsbury's Vin de Table (by then I might not even
have a table) then, of course, I will have to come
grovelling to you, my fixer, saying (in a Brooklyn accent)
"give us a break, I've gotta have the money for another
fix of Chateau Latour 1947".   Of course, by then I will
be totally within your power.

In return I am going to send you some flowers, I want you
to get hooked on cheap hybrid freesia so that one day **you**
will start grovelling to me saying "Spike freesia, I've got
to have freesia, give us a break will you"   So, even now
the battle to the death is one, as to who gets hooked
on what first.

I will come up and pay you a visit one evening, you will
recognise me, I will be the one with the hyperdermic full

/Contd..

Paul Getty Junior loved receiving letters from Spike. He'd write to Spike just to receive a reply.

of Chateau Latour, which I will be mainlining into my
throat.

I have just been reading Gershwins Years by Edward Jablonski
and it gives an amazing feeling of the virility of America
between 1918 - 1937.   I could not help feeling that the
opportunities presented to George and Ira Gershwin could
not exist today, and I am trying to figure out why.

I have got a great idea, why don't we lease your father's
Pompeian Villa at Malibu to McDonald's, and we could quote
"Genuine Pompeian Big Mac and Chips, by Pliny the
Younger", and how about McDonalds Pompeian Volcanic
Holocaust Special, and finally, when are you going to
admit that you really are Howard Hughes.

Love, light and peace,

Spike Milligan.

P.S. Try and get a cassette of Gershwin's Piano Concerto
in 'F', which really represented America's break out
into the classical world.

9 Orme Court,
LONDON. W. 2.

23rd March, 1984

Paul Getty Jnr.,
Son of Famous Piano Carrying Father,
Tudor House,
16 Cheyne Walk,
LONDON. S.W.3.

My dear Paul,

Seeing that you knew what it was like to have shit
thrown at you from a crowd of Gooks, I am sending you
a copy of books of war poems.
I belong to this Trust, and it is basically an attempt
to get collections of poetry from soldiers, from ordinary
G.I'S, up to Generals, some good some bloody awful.
Nevertheless, it's an insight into the state of men's
minds under duress.
Amongst this batch you will find one of my own brilliant,
super poems which makes Siegfried Sassoon fifty times
better.
Anyhow, thought you might be interested.

Love, light and peace,

Spike Milligan.

9 Orme Court,
LONDON. W. 2.

6th December, 1983

George Harrison Esq.,
26 Cadogan Square,
LONDON. SW1X. 0JP.

Dear George,

You once said to me - the world is full of
arseholes, and I'm not one of them.   I have a
love for certain people and I have one for you,
but by sheer lack of contact it's running out.
I phone you frequently and never get a reply.
This is what you do, it's very simple; you
stand in front of a telephone and you insert
your fingers in the holes and carry out a series
of numbers which have been given to you.   Of
course, if you are rich you have buttons, which
Irishmen usually sew on their coats.
Of course, if you are extremely rich you don't
have to get in touch with anybody, and that's what
I am worried about.   The funeral takes place
at Golders Green Crematorium, no flowers please,
just money.   You will recognise me, I am the
dead one.

                    Love, light and peace,

                    Spike Milligan.

P.S.   Thank you for sending the letter about the

                                    /Contd..

Fender Guitar, believe it or not, I'm now playing
the Guitar, and the silly bastards who insure it
want living proof that it was a George Harrison
Guitar, and I said to them, it was a George Harrison
Guitar, but it is now mine.

9 Orme Court,
LONDON. W. 2.

12th January, 1984

Mr. & Mrs. P. McCartney,
MPL Communications Limited,
1 Soho Square,
LONDON. W.1.

Dear Paul & Linda,

Briefly, this is about the World you live in.   As
you know Greenpeace were responsible for finding the
high radiation level off the coast near Windscale.
They found it out for the human race, they did it
for free, because of it, as you know the Government
have closed the beach down.
For their trouble they are now going to be fined
£50,000 in the Law Courts, and to pay this they are
offering 64 shares, at £1,000 each in the vessel
Cedarlea.   I have bought one, would you like to,
for the sake of the human race.
Do let me know.

                              Love, light and peace,

                              Spike Milligan.

Out with the begging bowl for the Beatles.

1 Soho Square · London W1V 6BQ · Telephone 01-439 6621 · Telex 21294

26th January 1984

Spike Milligan
9 Orme Court
London W2.

Dear Spike,

It is good to have people like you in the world.

Not only would we like one share of the Greenpeace boat at £1,000, but we would like one each - so that's two please!

Do let us have full details as soon as you can.

love,

Paul & Linda McCartney

9 Orme Court,
LONDON. W. 2.

26th January, 1984

Mr. & Mrs. Paul McCartney,
MPL Communications Ltd.,
1 Soho Square,
LONDON. W1V. 6BQ.

My dear Paul and Linda,

In this lonely fight people like you are a light in
the darkness.
I tell you I have written to millionaires, and only
two boys in the 'Pop' world, Elton John and yourselves
have offered money.
Remember it's for your kids sake, and I don't know
of a better investment, do you?

                              Love, light and peace,

                              Spike Milligan.

P.S.   I am sending Linda a pound, to help pay
       the fine.

9 Orme Court,
LONDON. W. 2.

5th December, 1983

David Waddington Q.C., M.P.,
Minister of State,
Home Office,
50 Queen Anne's Gate,
LONDON. S.W.1.

Dear Mr. Waddington,

I am a Citizen of Eire; I used to be British but I
lost my citizenship, after fighting seven years in
the British Army, because somebody passed a Bill, and
any son born of an Irish father, who was born before
a certain date in Ireland was made Stateless.
As I have married a British wife, can I claim British
citizenship now?

                    Sincerely,

                    Spike Milligan.

SM/NF

He was determined to keep up the pressure about his citizenship.

N Fannes
9 Orme Court
Saudi - Bayswater
London W2

The S.M. Postal Clerking Service

1983. He saw it coming.

9 Orme Court,
LONDON. W. 2.

1st August, 1983

Nick Curnow Esq.,
Phillips,
65 George Street,
EDINBURGH.

Dear Nick,

This is to confirm our telephone conversation that
I will bid £6,200 for 'IN THE MIRROR'.
My contact will be my Manager, Norma Farnes, the late
Lady Calthorpe.   Will you please contact her, she
has Power of Attorney over everything in my life
except the Execution Squad.

                    Sincerely,

                    Spike Milligan.

DONT SEND — GO.

I went to Edinburgh. He didn't get his painting. He was devastated.

AUSTRALIAN NEWSPAPERS.   8/12/83.

RUMOURS OF MY DEATH ARE BASED
UPON SIMPLE FACT. RECENT NIGHTS I
HAVE TAKEN TO SLEEPING IN A
6'OO' DEEP GRAVE. I HAVE FOUND THIS
HAS GREATLY REDUCED MY OVERHEADS AND
TAXES, AND PEOPLE ARE NOW FEELING
GENUINELY SORRY FOR ME. EACH MORNING
ON RISING CRIES OF "TIS A MIRACLE"
GOES AROUND LONDON.
OTHERWISE APART FROM A YOUNG LADY
CALLED MURIEL BODY I AM QUITE WELL.
                    SPIKE MILLIGAN

                Sent 8/12/83
            AUSTRALIAN ASSOC' PRESS

An Australian newspaper reported his death.

The bubble reads: 'If my nose gets any bigger its going to take over.'

9 Orme Court,
LONDON. W. 2.

21st February, 1984

Cliff Morgan Esq.,
British Broadcasting Corporation,
Kensington House,
Richmond Way,
LONDON. W.14.

My dear Cliff,

You must be dead, prior to this letter I have been trying to
get in touch with you through a Welsh medium.
Briefly, the football Dodos are still stuffing in football
scores during rugby matches, although they have changed the
style. It was appalling, they gave nine football results
in the first half of the Ireland/England match, and yet
during the five minute interval, when they could have put the
entire half time football results on they did nothing. Really
Cliff, this is plain bloody stupid, surely you are not running
a bloody stupid organisation. They really are the bitter
end, and in this case, living evidence of it, is as I have
just explained.
Phone me and apologise for Wales beating Ireland, and (b)
phone me and I will tell you that France were very lucky to
got away with it. Wales has all the makings of a splendid
team. There was a disarming moment when they were on the
French line, during the last ten minutes, when a more mature
team would have scored, but by God the Welsh fire is being

/Contd..

Spike's hero: Spike was, in his own words, such a 'rugger bugger'.

232

stoked up again.   It must have raised the hopes of Wales
to see that performance.

I suggest, like always, the Irish will not beat Scotland,
against all the odds; so far my predictions have been
right, it was France, Scotland, and then a scrabble for
third place.

          Yours, still mad about the game.

               Spike Milligan.
          Dictated over the telephone and
          signed in his absence.

9 Orme Court,
LONDON. W. 2.

21st March, 1984

G.A. Griffiths Esq.,
District Works Officer,
Department of the Environment,
Buckingham Palace,
LONDON. S.W.1.

Dear Mr. Griffiths,

re: STREET LANTERNS IN
CONSTITUTION HILL.

Many years ago I was instrumental in preventing the street
lights in Constitution Hill being pulled down; primarily
because I discovered they were, in fact, the last in
London with circular lanterns, in whose light possibly
five generations of Monarchs had driven.
Alas, they were then converted from gas into what I believe
orange sodium lighting, which gave off a hideous glare,
and the Department was then forced to have frosted glass
put into the lanterns.   Everybody thinks this was a
colossal mistake, and I did write originally to the
Department and I got back a wishy washy letter stating
"the whole of the lighting system in London is going to
be re-investigated", I didn't know quite what that meant, but
the appalling orange sodium lighting remains in Constitution
Hill.
Both Prince Philip, and just three weeks ago, Prince Charles
said "can you please try and do something about this
lighting".
Originally I had said that the best method of conversion

/Contd..

His preservation mode.

234

would have been the green sodium lighting (I think that's
the term) which you find in Regent's Park, adjacent to
the Nash Terraces; this gives the effect of the original
gas lighting, and does not dazzle on coming drivers.
I am sending a copy of this letter to Prince Philip and
Prince Charles, so if you receive a personal visit from
them do not be mystified.
I wonder if you would consider this suggestion.   I
appreciate the difficulty of the financial costs, but
as I pointed out, everybody is dis-satisfied with the
effect of the lighting in Constitution Hill.
My warm regards.

                         Sincerely,

                         Spike Milligan.

9 Orme Court,
LONDON. W. 2.

3rd April, 1984

H.R.H. The Prince of Wales, K.G., K.T.,
Buckingham Palace,
LONDON. S.W.1.

Dear Prince Charles,

You will be getting a long bumpf letter from
Mr. G.A. Griffiths, Department of the Environment,
all I asked him was could he change the orange
sodium lamps in Constitution Hill, to gas green
sodium lamps.
He could have just said yes or no, he hasn't, just
thought you would like to know.

Love, light and peace,

Spike Milligan.

Same letter to Prince Philip.

9 Orme Court,
LONDON. W. 2.

30th April, 1984

Michael Parkinson Esq.,
Lyndal Mount,
Fishery Road,
Bray,
BERKS.

Dear Michael,

I believe that you are taking over from poor Michael
Aspel, how can you put this poor father of four out of
work like this.

It's a coincidence that I have been asked to appear on
this programme to help the ratings, it means, of course,
that I will have to leave your poor mother in the work-
house for that day.

She still asks about you and yours, and thanks you for
the parcels of pile ointment.

Yours,

Nurse Milligan.

Amusing Michael Parkinson, or trying to.

10th April, 1984

The Editor,
Guardian,
119 Farringdon Road,
LONDON. E.C.1.

Dear Sir,

Help. My father was British, my grandfather was British,
my mother is British, and my brother is British, I <u>was</u>
British.   I served seven years in the army during the
last war.

In 1960 I went to renew my British Passport, and was told
I was no longer entitled to it, and in the words of the
chinless wonder at the counter I was "now Stateless".
Some idiotic law had been passed, and they said I could
re-apply. I was so incensed I didn't think a country
that treated me like this deserved me, so I became a
Citizen of Eire.

I have since tried to become a British Citizen again, but
have always been given a mass of forms to fill in, and told
to get in the queue. I found this appalling treatment,
but now I see that if you can run a certain distance in
world record time, and your father is British, you can get
a passport within ten days.   The jolly chap from the Home
Office on television last night said "we do grant passports
to people whose parents are British if they are particularly
talented".

Without sounding egotistical, I thought I was a talented
member of the society, having entertained it for some

/Contd..

He won't let go: he's now becoming an embarassment. He loved that.

30 years during which time I received the very first ever
British Writer's Television Award, and yet I still remain
 a foreigner.
I wrote to the Home Secretary personally over a week ago,
telling him they owed me a British Passport for my services
to this Country, so far dead silence. If I don't receive
a reply soon, you will see me training for the world
mile record which will, no doubt, guarantee me a passport.

                   Sincerely,

                   Spike Milligan.

9 Orme Court,
LONDON. W. 2.

10th May, 1985

The Editor,
Daily Mirror,
Holborn Circus,
LONDON. E.C.1.

Sir,

It was very touching to see the letter written by your
readers Brian and Pamela Dean regarding the way the
Home Office refused my British Passport, and despite a
letter to The Queen, Mrs. Thatcher and the Home Secretary
I am still treated at arms length, and the only way to
re-entry is to fill in forms and take an oath of allegiance
to the Queen.   I thought having risked my bloody life for
five years in the last war was sufficient evidence to
prove my loyalty.
I have not given up the fight, I am currently enquiring as
to how Yehudi Menhuin was given a British Passport without
having to go through the normal channels, as quoted in The
Times.
All the flag waving and speech making on V.E. Day didn't
mean a thing to me, I just felt I didn't belong to this
anymore, and it is a very sad state of affairs to arrive at.
Thank you Great Britain; no wonder the natives asked us
to leave India.   Mind you, half of them are now British
Citizens - see you in Australia folks, they like me out
there.

Sincerely,

Keep it up, Spike.

240

9 Orme Court,
LONDON. W. 2.

10th May, 1985

The Rt. Hon. Leon Brittan, Q.C., M.P.,
Secretary of State for the Home Office,
50 Queen Anne's Gate,
LONDON. S.W.1.

Dear Mr. Brittan,

I notice in The Times (3rd May) Yehudi Menhuin a Swiss
National has been given British Nationality, and to
quote him "did not have to make an official application
to the Home Office, the details of which are confidential".
Does this present a fresh opportunity for me to be granted
British Citizenship without the necessity of going through
the procedure, which as you know I find extraneous; having
proved my loyalty to the Crown having served five years
in the British Army, and apart from which being a member of
20 sterling British organisations, many of which I am
Vice President like the British Trust for Conservation
Volunteers – but no longer being British I ought to resign.
I wonder if there is any new light in this stupid dark
bureaucratic tunnel.

Yours sincerely,

Spike Milligan.

Now it's the Secretary of State's turn.

9 Orme Court,
LONDON. W. 2.

7th June, 1985

The Rt. Hon. Leon Brittan, Q.C., M.P.,
Secretary of State for the Home Office,
50 Queen Anne's Gate,
LONDON. SW1H. 9AT.

Dear Leon,

Thank you for your letter, you sound a decent enough chap.
O.K. so the "Times" article was misleading (God save us
from our misleading newspapers).
I was brought up on the principle of the Socratic argument,
there can only be one truth, and that sometimes is outside
of the law.   I am still totally baffled as to having been
born British, to British parents, living as a British person
in England for most of my life, partly in India, serving
the British Crown - one moment I am British and then at the
stroke of a pen I am not British.   You see I don't mind
the law being an ass, but being a total bloody fool is
another thing.
What galls me, dear Leon, is the fact that having risked my
life in the service of the Crown and proved my loyalty in
more than 100 ways, I find it galling that I should be put
in the position of asking to take the Oath of Allegiance
to the Queen; which can only mean up to that stage I have
not been allegiant to the Queen, that can be the only
process of that ceremony.   It's rather like a constable
seeing a man shoot a person dead and then arresting the
corpse for being murdered. I find this allegiance to the
Queen ceremony as demeaning, by that degree of logic.
In referring to the law that brought this ridiculous situation
about, I cannot see what the vista was in creating this dis-
possession of a person's British nationality, I can't see
any rationale in it at all, if it was an attempt to stop
the flood gates of immigration, as you know this failed

/Contd..

miserably.

Once again on the Socratic argument of truth, it seems strange you yourself being Semitic by descent are the Home Secretary, whereas I who have Scottish, English and Irish blood, and therefore, much more British ethnically, am really not British. It's as Alice said "It's all very strange".

However, I know you are a kindly man and a gentleman and if you are very very good you might get invited to have dinner at my place - that is, I hope you do not mind dining with foreigners.

I give you my warm regards because of you personally bending over backwards for me to become British - but wait - another thought, if I have to pay £55 to get a British Passport why did they not give me £55 for it when they took it away from me?

My word, didn't we Australians give you Pommies a thrashing in the two one day cricket matches.

Love, light and peace,

Spike Milligan.

The pure logic of £55. And when did he become an Australian?

LORD BERNSTEIN, LL.D. *President*

GRANADA GROUP LIMITED

Granada Television
Granada T V Rental
Granada Theatres
Granada Publishing
Granada Motorway Services
Barranquilla Investments
Novello Music

36 Golden Square London WIR 4AH   Telephone: 01-734 8080 Telegrams: Granada London

2nd July 1985

Dear Spike,

I have your 'exploratory' letter of 20th June and on the strength of that letter I have persuaded my TV Rental colleagues to give you the black and white portable Sony TV with their love and good wishes.

Mr David Parish, one of GTVR's top bosses, will turn this note into official bumpf any day.

It was good to hear from you.

As ever,

Sidney

Mr Spike Milligan,
9 Orme Court,
London W2

10/JM/PPL

20 June letter – lost. Spike wrote, 'I've rented my TV too long; it's about time you gave it to me.' Lord Bernstein's reply.

9 Orme Court,
London W 2.

17th July 1985.

The Lord Bernstein LLD,
Granada Group Ltd,
36 Golden Square,
London W1.

Dear Sidney,

Thank you for speaking up for Granada so bravely. Believe
it or not my manager has just asked me to sign a petition
to the Soviet Ambassador saying Anatoly Shcharansky should
be allowed to join his wife Avital in Israel; so you can tell
I am partially converted, which is how my last mini metro
sounded when I was driving.
I must tell you that the letter was really sent in the spirit
of a joke trying to break your day to day mundane inflow of
mail.
Anyhow looking at the set this very minute, and I see to my
horror it's gone on the blink, do you have exorcist powers?

                    Love, light and peace.

                    Spike Milligan,

Yr letter dated 3 Oct ~~arrived~~ arrived today 9 october.
. I'm replying at once

My dear Norma –
    Business letter.

1) Phantom. ~~Raspberry~~ blower'. Keep it on ice till I get
back. Peter Sellers once said hed like to do it
as a film. So I'll investigate that channel - as it would
be more lucrative as a film..

2) Goon Record. In the Goons there are numerous occassions
where either P. Sellers - or my self play a chord or our
own tune on the piano, can they find one such occassion -
and put that on the end. ~~in place of~~ I'm in no rush to
get it on by christmas - But I want to get it right -
. they just want to rush it - in Gropes of money. Believe
me, no matter when they issue it - it will sell
well - anytime. So let them stew. '

3) ~~Duncan Woods~~ - Beachcomber TV. I want to see
the script - became Barry Took has never written
anything on his own - hes always had a co
writer - and I dont think he can write good
. stuff on his own.

4) D Sellinger - Film. Sounds OK – . depends on
Oblomov – (I dont think its going to happen) Film world
is much more lucrative. Tell him (Dennis) to carry on as
tho' Oblomov didn't exist. I'd like to see script.

Sending me a pressed flower. What did he want me to do that I know I wouldn't have wanted to do?

246

Julie Felix show

1) Is it a variety show with audience?
If so, you can't go on and read
childrens poetry — you <u>have</u> to do an
act — with a proper ending

2) If its just a studio show — then
I can do a more 'literary act'. ie
Reading from 'Puckeroo' or the like.

3) How many minutes

4) Is there an Orchestra

5) OK I'll talk to Oofman when I
return

Jimmy Verner — 1) I am only doing this tour — because
there was no other continuous work
available —, 2) I have only <u>agreed</u>
(not signed) to do Bradford — 3 weeks
in Dublin — and a promise to David
Conyers to do Blackpool (as I had not
done the ~~Blackpool the~~ Blackpool week they
were expecting me to do) after that —
nothing.
Loosing Phanthem Rasberry blow — is a bit
of a financial shock — I was using that
show to fill in Work over December —
so I'll have to complete the Current
Bed-Sit Tour — Bradford — Dublin — Blackpool — no

agreed dates till I get back – and see what real
work exists – because promises, in this proffession, rarely
become reality [Like the bird who gave me Champagne –
and wanted one to make a film of London Buildings]

Now are there any Pantommimes going – ?̶S̶t̶h̶h̶b̶b̶N̶e̶l̶s̶o̶n̶
Ask Bernard Delfont – he likes me
Ohes must limited 8 week runs like – Golders Green – ?
limited because of Oblomov –
↑This Oblomov is a bloody nuisance – its holding me
back. – Can you phone Cindy Daggine and ask
her how near to a reality is Broadway? –
PS. If I was offered a Big Panto, long run, good money (like
Palladium) – Then take it – Oblomov will have to wait.

I have a deal to put on Bed-Sit
here in Sydney. – Tell you about it when
I come back.

Needless to say BMC never ever
phoned me to say 'No Car' – I wanted
4 days – (Twit) then I did a TV-
interview – in exchange they have
given me a car free for the holiday
– Tell the gentlemen at BMC – England
Thanks for nothing – especially the
indifference – good so I can read the future

I _knew_ there would be no Car.

I promise 2oo Cigarettes.

I'll let you know the Flight etc.

Give Eric my regards - tell him lets get together when I return,

. SUN!. SUN ! Sea -
Beaches — Mountains
Flowers — Women must
Big . !!. And

Wine (Iced!)

As Ever
Spike

9 Orme Court
Bayswater
London W2 4RL

Rt Hon Tony Blair
Prime Minister
10 Downing Street
London
SW1A 2AA

July 24th 1997

Dear Tony,

Whilst you are doing so much for the human race would you
spare a thought for those fur bearing animals. That's all.

LOve,light and peace,

SPIKE MILLIGAN

We agreed some time later. He thought about neither.

Spike Milligan

9 Orme Court
Bayswater
London
W2 4RL

Fax To:Daily Mail
        Letters Page
        Northcliffe House
        2 Derry Street
        London W8 5TT
        0171-937-7493

August 5th 1998

Sir,

I was horrified that the Roman Catholic religion refused to
bury Eva Bartok. The Message Jesus gave to Mary Magdalene
was 'Go and sin no more' - an act of forgiveness which
apparently the Roman Catholic church are bypassing.

                        Yours horrified catholic,

                        Spike

                        SPIKE MILLIGAN

Spike Milligan

Fax:0171-782-5046

9 Orme Court
Bayswater
London
W2 4RL

The Editor
The Times
News International
1 Virginia Street
London
E1 9BD

September 21st 1998

Sir,

What Foreign Office idiot sent the Queen to a riot
infested country. One day they will get it right.

Sincerely,

Spike

SPIKE MILLIGAN

Nothing changes.

Dear Jack + Norma,

Im a bit overwhelmed by magnificent and generous birthday present it was more than a present it was like a dowery, if S control myself it will last till my next birthday, the question is will S.

Love
Spike

Im glad S got it out of the office before Jack spotted it!

In his later years his favourite wine was an Australian Burgundy, Grange Hermitage, which cost an arm and a leg. We bought him six bottles for his 75th birthday.

The End